Nancy Clark's

Food Guide for Marathoners

Tips for Everyday Champions

Meyer & Meyer Sport

DEDICATION

I dedicate this book to the marathoners who give of their time and energy to raise money for important causes; they help make the world a better place. May the information in this book help these everyday champions enjoy high energy, good health and "smooth running" throughout their training and the marathon itself.

British Library Cataloguing in Publication Data
A catalogue record for this book is available from the British Library

Nancy Clark's Food Guide for Marathoners
Maidenhead: Meyer & Meyer Sport (UK) Ltd., 2007
ISBN 978-1-84126-322-9

© 2007 by Meyer & Meyer Sport (UK) Ltd.
4th, revised Edition 2011
Auckland, Beirut, Budapest, Cairo, Cape Town, Dubai, Graz, Indianapolis, Maidenhead,
Melbourne, Olten, Singapore, Tehran, Toronto
Member of the World
Sports Publishers' Association (WSPA)
www.w-s-p-a.org
Printed and bound by: B.O.S.S Druck und Medien GmbH, Germany
ISBN 978-1-84126-322-9
E-Mail: info@m-m-sports.com
www.m-m-sports.com

Nancy Clark's Food Guide for Marathoners

Contents

Foreword

During my 40+ years of running and 30+ years of coaching, I've come to appreciate the role of nutrition in fitness, sport, and long-term health. I've consulted with a number of nutritional experts in this period. I've not found anyone more knowledgeable or more experienced in working with runners than Nancy Clark. When the right foods are eaten, at the right time, recovery time is reduced, energy is sustained, and the muscles work better. An even greater psychological boost occurs due to proper ingestion of fluids and blood sugar boosting foods. Nancy's proven advice will also bestow an added level of confidence, which reduces stress and improves performance.

Nancy's advice is based upon solid research. She studies the new findings and knows the trends. For decades, she has advised thousands of runners and solved thousands of nutritional problems. I believe that Nancy's articles are so popular because she covers the issues thoroughly but explains the concepts in easy-to-understand language. She tells you what she knows will work, from a deep well of experience and intelligence.

Nancy is a runner and a marathoner. She's put her advice to the test, and fine-tuned it on the roads. I highly recommend this book.

Jeff Galloway

Preface

"I've got a good training program, but nutrition is my missing link," reported David, a novice marathoner who recognized he could have far better stamina and endurance if he could only manage to eat better. David's story is familiar to many of my clients who have the dedication to train but just cannot seem to muster the same dedication to stick to their desired nutrition program. Somehow "eating well" can become difficult as marathoners spend more and more time training, stretching and recovering from their long walks or runs.

And then there are the novice marathon finishers who want to do yet another marathon so they have the chance to learn from their mistakes. As Jessica, a two-time marathoner reported: I started running a year ago. I ran the L.A. marathon in 5:19, and I learned a lot from that first marathon. I next ran the San Francisco Marathon in 4:52. I was on pace for a 4:30 marathon, but I hit the wall at mile 20 … I know I didn't eat right. So now, I want to know:

- Am I eating the right foods on a daily basis?
- What should I eat for snacks?
- What can I do about the hungry horrors at 4:00 in the afternoon?
- What should I eat during my long runs?
- What's the best way to carbo-load?
- Would I be a better runner if I were lighter?
- If so, how can I lose weight and still have energy to exercise?

Like many marathoners, Jessica's workday was a marathon in itself! She started her day with an early morning run (5:30 to 6:30 a.m.) and ended with rushing home from work to cook dinner for her family. She barely grabbed breakfast and lunch, so as soon as she walked in the door to her kitchen, she started devouring almonds by the handful and grapes by the bunches. She'd hoped that running would result in the loss of her undesired body fat, but the fat failed to "melt away," much to her dismay.

Jessica came to me frustrated, filled with questions, and eager to learn how to eat better, fuel her muscles optimally, and enjoy not only higher energy but also better training runs and a faster third marathon. I assured her I could help her reach her goal. I reminded Jessica—and all aspiring marathoners such as yourself—that, while training is an important part of your marathon preparation, proper fueling is equally important. If you don't make the time to eat wisely and well, you might as well hang up your dream of flying through the marathon with energy to spare! But, if you take to heart the information in this *Food Guide for Marathoners* and practice eating wisely (as well as training wisely), you'll be far more likely to have a satisfying marathon experience.

With best wishes for miles of high energy, smiles, and wonderful memories,

Nancy Clark, MS, RD
Certified Specialist in Sports Dietetics (CSSD)
Healthworks Fitness Center
1300 Boylston Street
Chestnut Hill, MA, 02467
www.nancyclarkrd.com

Acknowledgements

With sincere thanks and appreciation to:

Hans Meyer, Thomas Stengel and Kathrin Albrecht for their publishing help. Kerstin Vonderbank for designing a nice-looking book.

Photographers Bob Fitzgerald, Tommy Owens, Tom Dooley, Bruce Zavodny, Jim Newsom, Will Arts, Kate Carter

Larry Armstrong, PhD for granting permission to use the Urine Color Chart.

My husband John McGrath, for his ever-available help, support, and love.

My children, John Michael and Mary, for their interest and abundant suggestions.

My running buddies, Jean Smith and Catherine Farrell, for keeping me on my toes.

My clients, many of whom are marathoners, for sharing their experiences and teaching me how to better help other marathoners with similar struggles.

The many participants in the Team in Training Marathon training programs as well as other marathon training programs. They are inspirational!

Chapter 1

Day-to-Day
Eating for Health
and High Energy

"I've got my training down, but my eating needs help," reported Jeff, a novice marathoner who recognized his sport diet left a lot to be desired. He generally ate on the run, skipped breakfast, skimped on fruit, rarely ate vegetables, and munched on too much "junk food" at night. Once he started running for longer than 12 miles, he lagged on energy and felt horrible at the end of his long runs. He knew inadequate eating was the root of the problem and came to me, a sports dietitian, to help him find the solution.

Fueling yourself well on a daily basis requires time-management skills. You need to learn how to manage to find time to:

- food shop so you'll have wholesome sports foods available.
- fuel up and refuel at the right times.

In this chapter, I'll share with you the basic tips about how to eat well, even when you are eating on the run and even if you are not much of a cook. But first, it helps to understand my definition of "eating well." My simple definition is to–

1. Eat at least three kinds of wholesome foods at each meal
2. Eat two kinds of wholesome foods at each snack.
3. Eat on a time line—even-sized meals throughout the day, as opposed to crescendo-eating (a small breakfast and a belly-stuffing meal at the end of the day).
4. Choose to eat at least 90 percent of the calories from quality foods and, if desired, the remaining 10 percent from sweets and treats.

Because many of today's marathoners prefer to spend time training rather than

Some Top Sports Foods

Many marathoners don't have time to cook or prepare foods. Here are some readily available, ready-to-eat, nutrient-dense sports foods to help you easily enjoy a top sports diet.

Some of the best fruits for vitamins A and/or C:
oranges, grapefruit, mango, bananas, melons, berries, kiwi

Some of the best vegetables for vitamins A and/or C:
broccoli, spinach, green and red peppers, tomatoes, carrots, sweet potato, winter squash

Easy sources of calcium for strong bones:
lowfat milk, yogurt, cheese; calcium-fortified orange juice, soy milk, and tofu

Convenient pre-cooked (or no-cook) proteins for building and protecting muscles:
Deli roast beef, ham, and turkey, canned tuna and salmon, hummus, peanut butter, tofu, cottage cheese, canned beans (pinto, kidney, garbanzo)

Cook-free grains for carbohydrates and fiber:
High-fiber breakfast cereals (preferably iron-enriched), wholesome breads and bagels, whole-grain crackers

Dietary Recommendations for Good Health

By following these dietary recommendations, you can substantially reduce your risk of developing heart disease and other diseases of aging.
- Balance calorie intake and physical activity to achieve and maintain a healthy body weight.
- Consume a diet rich in vegetables and fruits.
- Choose whole-grain, high-fiber foods.
- Consume fish, especially oily fish, at least twice a week.
- Limit your intake of saturated fat to < 7% of energy, trans fat to < 1% of energy, and cholesterol to < 300 mg per day by
  —choosing lean meats and vegetable alternatives.
  —selecting fat-free (skim), 1%-fat, and lowfat dairy products.
  —minimizing intake of partially hydrogenated fats.
- Minimize your intake of beverages and foods with added sugars
- Choose and prepare foods with little or no salt
- If you consume alcohol, do so in moderation.
- When you eat food that is prepared outside of the home, follow these dietary recommendations.

Source: Diet and Lifestyle Recommendation Revision 2006: A Scientific Statement From the American Heart Association Nutrition Committee. A. Lichtenstein et all. Circulation 2006; 114:82-96.

cooking, take note: You don't have to be a good cook to eat well. You just need to be a smart shopper. I'll help you with that!

To help guide optimal food choices, many countries and health organizations have created dietary guidelines. The United States' guidelines describe a healthy diet as one that emphasizes fruits, vegetables, whole grains, and fat-free or lowfat milk and milk products; includes lean meats, poultry, fish, beans, eggs, and nuts; and is low in saturated fats, trans fats, cholesterol, salt (sodium), and added sugars. More specifically, this is what you want to keep in mind as you make your daily food choices:

- Try to eat at least two cups of fruit and 2 1/2 cups of vegetables per day (This is the reference for a 2,000-calorie intake; most marathoners need more calories than that and could wisely consume some of those extra calories from fruits and vegetables.)
- Choose a variety of colors of fruits and vegetables each day: red apples, green peppers, orange carrots, white potatoes...
- Enjoy whole-grain products at least two times per day, such as oatmeal for breakfast and whole wheat bread for lunch. The rest of the recommended grains can come from enriched grain products, such as enriched pasta. In general, at least half the grains should come from whole grains. (Whole grains include wheat, rice, oats, corn, and barley.)
- Drink 24 ounces (3 cups; 720 ml) per day of fat-free or lowfat milk or yogurt, or the calcium-equivalent in lowfat cheese (8 ounces of milk or yogurt = 240 ml = 1 cup = .75 ounces (20 g) of cheese).

- When selecting and preparing meat, poultry, dry beans, and milk or milk products, make choices that are lean, lowfat, or fat-free.
- Limit your intake of saturated and trans fats and choose healthier oils such as olive and canola oils, nuts and nut butters, and oily fish such as salmon.

Balancing Your Diet

The trick to balancing the recommended servings of foods during your day is to plan to have at least three out of five food groups per meal, and one or two food groups per snack, such as:

	Breakfast	Lunch	Snack	Dinner	Snack
Grain	oatmeal	bread		spaghetti	popcorn
Fruit	raisins	banana	apple		juice
Vegetable		baby carrots		tomato sauce	
			(lowfat)		
Dairy	milk	yogurt	cheese	parmesan	
Protein	almonds	peanut butter		ground turkey	

Carbohydrates for Your Sports Diet

By eating grains, fruits and vegetables as the foundation of each meal, you'll consume about 55 to 65 percent of your calories from carbohydrates. This is exactly what you need for a high-energy sports diet. These carbohydrates are stored in muscles in the form of glycogen, the energy you need to train hard day after day, and to compete well on race day.

Grain foods are a popular source of carbohydrates for most active people. But some marathoners believe they will get fat if they eat breads, cereals and pastas at each meal. False. Carbohydrates are not fattening; excess calories are fattening. (See Chapter 15: Weight and Marathoners) Your body needs carbs to fuel your muscles.

Fruits and vegetables are also great sources of carbohydrates. But eating the recommended two cups (500 g) of fruits and 2.5 cups (600 g) of vegetables is another story. As one marathoner sheepishly remarked, "I'm lucky if I eat that much in a week." The trick is to eat large portions. Most marathoners can easily enjoy a banana (1 cup fruit, 240 g) and 8 ounces (one cup, 240 ml) of orange juice in the morning. That's the minimal fruit duty for the day! A big bowl of salad filled with colorful tomatoes, carrots, and peppers can account for the minimal recommended 2.5 cups of vegetables.

If your goal is to be a strong runner in your golden years, today you want to start choosing meals abundant with fruits, vegetables and whole grain foods.

Fruits: Recommended Daily Intake—2 to 3 cups (500 to 700 g)
Each of these counts as one cup:

Orange Juice	8 ounces	240 ml
Apple	1 small	100 g
Banana	1 small	100 g
Caned Fruit	1 cup	240 g
Dried fruit	1/2 cup	80 g

Vegetables: Recommended Daily Intake—2.5 to 3 + cups (600 to 700 + g)
Each of these counts as one cup:

Broccoli	1 medium stalk	200 g
Spinach	2 cups raw	60 g
Salad Bar	1 average bowl	100 g
Spaghetti Sauce	1 cup	250 g

Fruits and vegetables are truly nature's vitamin pills, chock full of vitamin C (to help with healing), beta-carotene (to protect against cancer), fiber (to aid with regular bowel movements), and numerous other vitamins and minerals. The sidebar, Eat More Veggies! (page 14), offers suggestions for ways to boost your veggie intake simply.

Protein for Your Sports Diet

Like carbohydrates, protein-rich foods are also an important part of your sports diet. You should eat a protein-rich food at each meal. Marathoners tend to either over- or underconsume protein, depending on their health consciousness and lifestyle. Whereas some marathoners frequently choose pepperoni pizza, fast food burgers and other meals filled with saturated fats, other marathoners bypass these foods in their efforts to eat a lowfat or vegetarian diet—but they neglect to replace beef with beans. For additional information and guidelines see Chapter 6: Protein for Marathoners.

 I've found that keeping with me a cooler packed with wholesome foods allows me to graze often and eat the items that fit my dietary requirements. To simplify the process of getting my trough ready, I choose pre-cut fruits and vegetables, dried fruits, nuts, energy bars, yogurt, etc. If I had to work hard at preparing these foods, this plan would quickly fall off my priority list.

John Correia, San Diego, CA

Recommended daily protein intake: *5 to 7 ounces*
(or ounce-equivalents; 140 to 200 g)

Protein-rich Foods	Marathoner's Portion	Number of ounces or ounce-equivalents
Tuna	6 oz. (170 g) can drained	3-4 ounce-equivalents
Chicken	6-ounce breast	6
Peanut Butter	2-4 tablespoons	1-2
Kidney Beans	1 cup	4

Eat More Veggies!

If you struggle to consume the recommended two to three servings of vegetables per day, the following tips may help you enhance your vegetable intake—and your health.

- Eat more of the best vegetables, less of the rest. In general, dark green, deep yellow, orange, and red vegetables have far more nutrients than pale ones. Hence, if you dislike pale zucchini, summer squash, and cucumbers, don't work hard to acquire a taste for them. Instead, put your efforts into having more broccoli, spinach, and winter squash—the richly colored, more nutrient-dense choices.

- Eat colorful salads filled with tomatoes, green peppers, carrots, spinach, and dark lettuces. Pale salads with white lettuce, cucumbers, onions, celery, and other pale veggies offer little more than crunch. When smothered with dressing, this crunch becomes highly caloric. Alternatives to a pale restaurant salad include tomato juice, vegetable soup, a steamed veggie or, when you get home, a handful of raw baby carrots for a bedtime snack.

- Fortify spaghetti sauce with a (frozen) chopped broccoli or green peppers. Steam or microwave the veggies before you add them to the tomato sauce.

To meet your protein requirement for the day, you should consume a protein-rich food at each meal. Lowfat dairy foods such as milk, yogurt and cheese (or other calcium-rich foods, such as calcium-fortified soy milk) offer a good way to boost your intake of high quality protein as well as calcium. Calcium is important not only for growing teens and women who want to optimize bone density, but also men who want to have strong bones past the age of 70. For only 300 calories, all marathoners can easily contribute towards their protein intake plus achieve the recommended two to three servings of calcium-rich foods per day by consuming:

- 8 oz. (240 ml) of milk or soy milk on breakfast cereal
- 8 oz. (240 ml) of yogurt with lunch
- a (decaf) latte made with lowfat milk for an afternoon energizer

When choosing dairy foods, note that fat-free and lowfat products are preferable for heart-health and calorie control, but you need not suffer with skim milk if you really don't like it. You can always cut back on fat in other parts of your diet. For example, Margie, a first-time marathoner, opted for cereal with reduced-fat (2%) milk (five grams of fat per cup), but saved on fat elsewhere in her diet by choosing lowfat cheese and mustard instead of mayonnaise on her sandwich. (For more information on dietary fat, see Chapter 7.)

Runners who prefer a dairy-free diet or are lactose intolerant should take special care to eat adequate amounts of nondairy calcium sources or lactose-free milk. See the sidebar, Calcium Equivalents (page 16), for food suggestions.

- Choose fast foods with the most veggies:
  - pizza with peppers, mushrooms, and extra tomato sauce
  - Chinese entrees stir-fried with vegetables
  - lunchtime V-8 juice instead of diet soda

- Even over-cooked vegetables are better than no vegetables. If your only option is over- cooked veggies from the cafeteria, eat them. While cooking does destroy some of the vegetable's nutrients, it does not destroy all of them. Any vegetable is better than no vegetable!

- Keep frozen vegetables stocked in your freezer, ready and waiting. They are quick and easy to prepare, won't spoil quickly, and have more nutrients than "fresh" vegetables that have been in the market and then your refrigerator for a few days. Because cooking (more than freezing) reduces a vegetable's nutritional content:
  - quickly cook vegetables only until tender crisp and use the cooking water as a broth
  - microwave vegetables in a covered dish
  - stir-fry them with a little olive oil.

- When all else fails, eat fruit to help compensate for lack of vegetables. The best alternatives include bananas, oranges, grapefruit, melon, berries, and kiwi. These choices are rich in many of the same nutrients found in vegetables.

Sweets and Treats

Some marathoners eat far too many sweets and treats, even though they know they should be eating a wholesome diet based on grains, fruits, and vegetables. If you have a sweet tooth, you may be able correct this imbalance by eating larger portions of wholesome foods before you get too hungry. Marathoners who get too hungry tend to choose sugary, fatty foods (such as apple pie, instead of apples). A simple solution to sweet cravings is to prevent hunger by eating more wholesome food at meals.

Take note: you need not eat a "perfect diet" (no fats, no sugar) to have a good diet. Nothing is nutritionally wrong with having a cookie for dessert after having eaten a sandwich, milk, and fruit for lunch. But a lot is wrong with skipping the sandwich and then eating cookies for lunch. That's when nutrition and performance problems arise.

The key to balancing fats and sugars appropriately in your diet is to abide the following guidelines:
- 10 percent of your calories can come from refined sugar, if desired (about 200–300 calories from sugar per day for most marathoners)
- 25 percent of your calories can appropriately come from fat (about 450–750 calories from fat per day, or roughly 50–85 grams of fat per day)

Hence, moderate amounts of chips, cookies, and ice cream can fit into an overall healthful food plan.

Calcium Equivalents

The recommended daily calcium intake is:

Age Group	Calcium (mg)
Teens, 9-18 years	1,300
Adults, 19-50 years	1,000
Adults, 51 + years	1,200

Source: Dietary Reference Intakes, National Academy of Science, 1997

The following foods all provide about 300 milligrams of calcium. Three choices per day, or one at each meal, will contribute to meeting your calcium needs.

Calcium-rich Dairy Foods	Amount
milk, whole or skim	1 cup (240 ml)
yogurt	1 cup (230 g)
cheese	1 1/2 ounces (45 g)
cottage cheese	2 cups (450 g)
frozen yogurt	1 1/2 cups (150 g)

Proteins	
soy milk*	1 cup (240 ml)
tofu	8 oz. (1/2 cake; 250 g)
salmon, canned with bones	5 ounces (140 g)
sardines, canned with bones	3 ounces (85 g)
almonds	4 ounces (110 g)

Vegetables	
Broccoli, cooked	3 cups (550 g)
Collard or turnip greens, cooked	1 cup (150 g)
Kale or mustard greens, cooked	1 1/2 cups (220 g)

Calcium-fortified foods*	
Orange juice	8 ounces
Rice milk	8 ounces
Almond milk	8 ounces

Check label to be sure the food has added calcium

Need Some Help Shaping Up Your Diet?

If you want personalized dietary advice, I recommend that you seek professional advice from a registered dietitian (RD) who specializes in sports nutrition and, ideally, is Board Certified as a Specialist in Sports Dietetics (CSSD). To find a sports dietition in your area, use the referral networks art the American Dietetic Association's website (www.eatright.org) or the website of ADA's practice group of sports dietitians (www.SCANdpg.org). Or try googling "sports nutritionist" or "sports dietitian" in your city. You'll be glad you did! This personal nutrition coach can help you enjoy miles of smiles and years of good health.

Summary

Nutrition for marathoning is all about fueling with a purpose so you can then enjoy the benefits of high energy and good health. Your food goals are to eat at least three kinds of wholesome foods at each meal; at least two kinds of wholesome foods for each snack; evenly-sized meals about every four hours throughout the day (as opposed to "crescendo eating" with a small breakfast and a large meal at the end of the day); at least 90% of the calories from quality foods and, if desired, the remaining 10% from sweets and treats. You need not eat a "perfect diet" to have a good diet, but you do want to choose more of the best foods (wholesome grains, fruits, vegetables, lowfat dairy, lean meats, beans and plant-sources of protein) and less of the rest.

Recipes for Success: Vegetables 101: Basic Cooking Tips

Vegetables are nutrient-rich, but cooking can destroy some of their nutritional value. To get the most nutrients from your vegetables, handle them properly so they have minimal exposure to air, heat, water, and light—the four elements that reduce their nutritional value.

- To reduce exposure to air: Store fresh vegetables in plastic containers. Cook covered.
- To reduce exposure to heat: Store fresh vegetables in the refrigerator; minimize cooking time to enhance the flavor and nutritional value.
- To reduce exposure to water: Cook in minimal water, stir-fry, or microwave.
- To reduce exposure to light: Store in a dark place (inside the fridge!); cook in a covered pan.

Basic Steamed Vegetables

1. Wash vegetables thoroughly; prepare and cut into pieces keeping the skin or peel, if appropriate.
2. Put 1/2-inch inch (1 cm) water in the bottom of a pan that has a tight cover.
3. Bring the water to a boil. Add the vegetables. Or, put the vegetables in a steamer basket and put this in the saucepan with 1 inch (2 cm) of water.
4. Cover the pan tightly and cook over medium heat until the vegetables are tender crisp, about 3 minutes for spinach, 10 minutes for broccoli, 15 minutes for sliced carrots.
5. Drain the vegetables, reserving the cooking water for soup or sauces, or simply drink it as a broth.

If you wish to add some seasonings before or after cooking, here are some nice combinations:

Basil	Green beans, tomatoes, zucchini
Oregano	Zucchini, mushrooms, tomatoes, onions
Dill	Green beans, carrots, peas, potatoes
Cinnamon	Spinach, winter squash, sweet potatoes
Marjoram	Celery, greens
Nutmeg	Corn, cauliflower, green beans
Thyme	Artichokes, mushrooms, peas, carrots
Parsley	Sprinkled on any vegetable

Basic Microwaved Vegetables

Microwave cookery is perfect for vegetables because microwaves cook the veggies quickly and without water, thereby retaining a greater percentage of the nutrients than with conventional methods.

1. Wash the vegetables and cut them into bite-size pieces. Put them in a microwavable container with a cover.

2. Microwave until tender crisp; stir halfway through cooking, so they cook evenly. The amount of time will vary according to your particular microwave oven and the amount of vegetable you are cooking. Start off with three minutes for a single serving; larger servings take longer. The vegetables will continue cooking after you remove them from the oven, so plan that into your cooking time.

Basic Stir-fried Vegetables

Vegetables stir-fried until tender crisp are very flavorful, colorful, and nutritious, but they do have more calories than if steamed. If weight is an issue, be sure to add only a minimal amount of oil (olive, canola, sesame) to the cooking pan. Some popular stir-fry combinations include:

- Carrots, broccoli, and mushrooms
- Onions, green peppers, zucchini, and tomatoes
- Chinese cabbage, bok choy, and water chestnuts

1. Wash, drain well (to prevent the water from spattering when the vegetables are added to the hot cooking oil), and cut the vegetables of your choice into bite-sized pieces or 1/8-inch slices. Whenever possible, slice vegetables diagonally to increase the surface area; this allows for faster cooking. Try to make the pieces uniform so they will cook evenly.

2. Heat the skillet over high heat. Add 1 to 3 teaspoons of oil, just enough to coat the bottom of the pan. Optional: Add a slice of ginger root or some minced garlic, stir-frying for one minute to add flavor.

3. Add the vegetables that take longest to cook (carrots, cauliflower, broccoli); a few minutes later add the remaining ones (mushrooms, bean sprouts, cabbage, spinach). Constantly lift and turn the vegetables to coat them with oil.

4. Add a little bit of water (1/4 to 1/2 cup), then cover and steam the vegetables for 2 to 5 minutes. Adjust the heat to prevent scorching.

5. Don't overcrowd the pan. Cook small batches at a time.

6. Optional add-ins: soy sauce, stir-fried beef, chicken, tofu, rice, or noodles.

7. To thicken the juices, stir in a mixture of 2 teaspoons cornstarch diluted into 1 tablespoon water. Add more water or broth if this makes the sauce too thick.

Optional: Garnish with toasted sesame seeds, mandarin orange sections, or pineapple chunks.

Basic Baked Vegetables
If you are baking chicken, potatoes, or a casserole, you might as well make good use of the oven and bake the vegetables, too. Some popular suggestions include:

- Eggplant halves sprinkled with garlic powder
- Zucchini with onions and oregano
- Carrots with ginger
- Sliced sweet potato with apple

1. Put the vegetables (seasoned as desired) in a covered baking dish with a small amount of water, or wrap them in foil.

2. Bake at 350°F (175°C) for 20 to 30 minutes (depending on the size of the chunks) until tender crisp. Caution: With foil-wrapped vegetables, be careful when opening the foil. The escaping steam might burn you.

Adapted from: Nancy Clark's Sports Nutrition Guidebook, Fourth Edition (Human Kinetics, 2008)

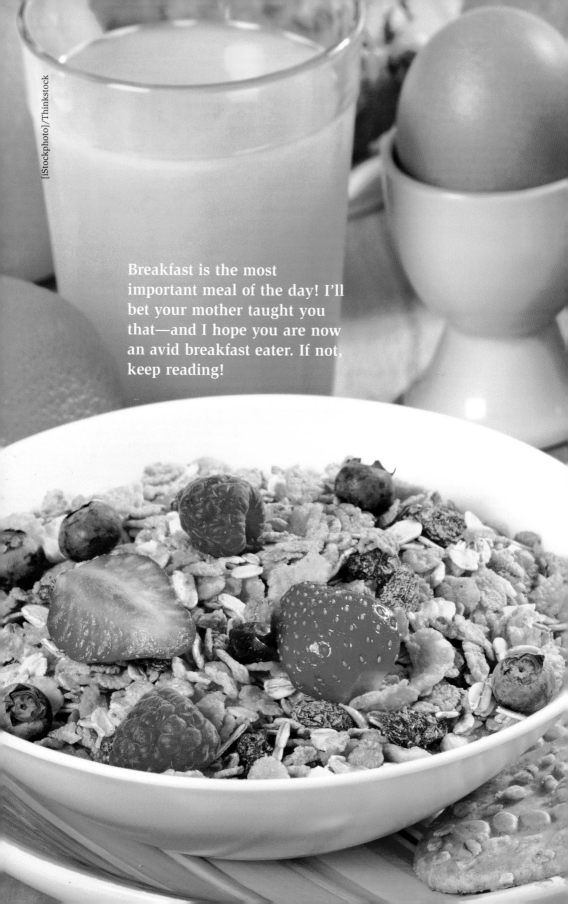

Breakfast is the most important meal of the day! I'll bet your mother taught you that—and I hope you are now an avid breakfast eater. If not, keep reading!

Breakfast:
The Meal of
Champions

Eating breakfast means you have to find the desire to do so. You'll want to eat breakfast is you observe that the benefits of eating a proper breakfast far outweigh the costs. Breakfast eaters tend to:

- eat a more nutrient-dense and overall better diet the rest of the day (a wholesome breakfast can reduce the urge for junk food at night)
- have lower blood cholesterol levels
- enjoy success with weight control (In one survey, 88% of dieters who lost weight and kept it off became religious breakfast eaters; only 4% rarely ate breakfast) (Wyatt, 2002).
- are mentally alert and more productive (just like school kids who eat breakfast)
- have more energy to enjoy exercise either in the morning or later that day.

As an athlete, you should eat even-sized meals about every four hours, starting with breakfast within three hours of waking. From petite female runners on a 2,000-calorie per day weight reduction diet, to tall men who devour 3,600 calories per day, marathoners require a hefty 500 to 900 calories for their morning fuel. (See Chapter 14 for information on how to calculate your calorie needs for breakfast and the entire day.)

 Breakfast was never my favorite meal of the day, but I soon learned it was essential to my overall endurance. My training sessions and times were markedly worse when I skipped breakfast. A bagel or cereal in the morning works wonders for me!

Shelley Smith, CO

Morning runners commonly split their breakfast into a pre-run snack, such as a banana, followed by the recovery meal, such as a bagel with peanut butter on their way to the office. By spending one-fourth of your calories in the morning, you have adequate energy to start your busy day, to say nothing of abate hunger and the 10:00 a.m. hungry horrors.

Despite my clear message about breakfast being the most important meal of the day, I have to coax my clients to experiment with eating (more) breakfast. Far too many marathoners under-eat in the morning. Some fear if they eat more at breakfast, they'll get fat. Or if they eat breakfast, they'll feel more hunger than if they abstain. Let's take at look at some standard breakfast excuses—and solutions.

I don't have time: Lack of priority is the real problem, not lack of time. If you can make time to train, you can make time to fuel for your training. Even if you choose to sleep to the last minute before dragging yourself out of bed, you can still choose to eat breakfast on the way to work. Breakfast need not be an elaborate occasion. You can quickly prepare a simple breakfast to eat on the run:

- a baggie filled with raisins, almonds, and granola.
- a wrap rolled with a slice or two of lowfat cheese
- a peanut butter and honey sandwich on wholesome bread
- a glass of milk, then a banana while walking to the bus or train

- a travel mug filled with a fruit smoothie or protein shake (there will always be coffee at the office)
- an energy bar and some grapes during the morning commute.

The key to breakfast on the run is to plan ahead. Prepare your breakfast the night before so that you can simply grab it and go during the morning rush. For example, on the weekends, you might want to make banana bread (see my favorite recipe at the end of this chapter) or buy a dozen bagels. Pre-slice the bread or the bagels, wrap the desired portion in individual plastic bags, and put them in the freezer. Take one out of the freezer at night so breakfast will be ready and waiting in the morning.

Breakfast interferes with my training schedule: If you are an early morning runner or walker (5:00-7:00 a.m.), you will likely exercise better and avoid an energy crash if you eat part of your breakfast before you exercise (assuming your stomach can tolerate food, of course). Coffee with extra milk, a swig of juice, half a bagel, or a slice of toast are popular choices that can get your blood sugar on the upswing, contribute to greater stamina, and help you feel more awake. If you prefer to abstain, at least have a hefty bedtime snack the night before to help bolster your morning blood sugar. (*Chapter 9: Fueling Before You Exercise* explains in greater detail the importance of morning food.)

> During training, we encourage our marathoners to start eating breakfast—even if they aren't breakfast people—to help prevent "the bonk." When someone bonks, we quiz them about what they ate that day. Inevitably, they have skipped breakfast. They learn to never do that again!
>
> *Coach, Matt Keil, San Jose, CA*

Breakfast is equally important if you exercise at mid-day or in the afternoon. You need to fuel up in order to do a quality workout that afternoon. Breakfast is essential if you are doing double workouts. Because your muscles are hungriest for carbohydrates within the first hour after hard exercise, a quick and easy recovery breakfast will set the stage for a strong second workout.

I sometimes hear marathoners express concern that eating breakfast interferes with their upcoming workout; that the food will sit heavily in the stomach or "talk back." This is unlikely. A lowfat meal at 7:00 to 8:00 a.m. (such as cereal and lowfat milk) should be well digested by noontime. Try it; you'll probably see a positive difference in your energy level.

I'm not hungry in the morning: If you have no morning appetite, the chances are you ate your breakfast calories the night before. Huge dinner? Ice cream? Too many cookies before bedtime? The solution to having no morning appetite is, obviously, to eat less at night so that you can start the day off hungry.

If running first thing in the morning "kills your appetite" (due to the rise in body temperature), keep in mind that you will be hungry within a few hours when you have cooled down. Plan ahead, so when the hungry horrors hit, you will have healthful options ready and waiting. Otherwise, you'll be likely to grab whatever's easy, which may include doughnuts, pastries and other high-fat foods.

I'm on a diet: Too many weight-conscious runners start their diet at breakfast. Bad idea. Breakfast skippers tend to gain weight and to be heavier than breakfast eaters. A satisfying breakfast prevents you from getting too hungry and overeating.

> I still find it hard to believe that when I started eating more at breakfast and lunch, I lost weight. I felt as though I was cheating all the time. My running times even improved because I was actually well-fueled instead of half-starved.

Laura Perkins,
New York City, NY

Your best bet for successful dieting is to eat during the day, burn off the calories, and then eat a lighter meal at night. See Chapter 15 for more weight loss details.

Breakfast makes me hungrier: Many marathoners complain that if they eat breakfast, they seem to get hungrier and eat more all day. This may result from thinking they have already "blown their diets" by eating breakfast, so they might as well keep overeating, then start dieting again the next day. Wrong.

Successful diets start at breakfast. If you feel hungry after breakfast you probably ate too little breakfast. For example, 100 calories of toast with jam is enough to whet your appetite but not to satisfy your calorie needs. Try budgeting about one-quarter of your calories for breakfast—500–600 calories for most 120–150 pound runners. This translates into two slices of toast with jam, a banana, lowfat yogurt, and juice; or yogurt and a bagel with peanut butter.

Note: If you overeat at breakfast, you can easily resolve the problem by eating less at lunch or dinner. You won't be as physically hungry for those meals and will be able to easily eat smaller portions.

The Breakfast of Champions

By now, I hope I've convinced you that breakfast is indeed the most important meal of the day for marathoners. What should you eat, you wonder? If you feel like cooking, enjoy hot oatmeal, French toast, or pancakes.

But if you are looking for a cook-free choice, I highly recommend cereal. Cereal is quick, convenient, and filled with the calcium, iron, carbohydrates, fiber, and other nutrients active people need. A bowl of bran cereal with fruit and lowfat milk provides a well-balanced meal that includes three of the five food groups (grain, milk, and fruit) and sets the stage for an overall lowfat diet.

Cereal is versatile. You can eat it dry if you're on the run, or preferably with lowfat milk and/or yogurt for a calcium booster. You can mix brands and vary the flavor with different toppings:

- sliced banana
- blueberries (a handful of frozen ones taste great—especially if microwaved)
- raisins
- canned fruit
- cinnamon
- maple syrup
- vanilla yogurt

My personal favorite is to put a mix of cereals in my bowl, top it with fruit, heat it in the microwave oven for 30 to 60 seconds, and then add cold milk. It's like eating fruit cobbler!

How to Choose the Best Breakfast Cereal

Needless to say, all cereals are not created equal. Some offer more nutritional value than others. Here are four tips to help you make the best choices.

Nontraditional Breakfasts

Not everyone likes cereal for breakfast, nor do they want to cook eggs or pancakes. If you are stumped by what to eat for breakfast, choose a food that you enjoy. After all, you'll be more likely to eat breakfast if it tastes good. Remember that any food—even a cookie (preferably oatmeal raisin, rather than chocolate chip)—is better than nothing. How about:

- **leftover pizza**
- **leftover Chinese food**
- **mug of tomato soup**
- **potato zapped in the microwave while you take your shower**
- **tuna sandwich**
- **peanut butter and apple**
- **protein bar**

1. *Choose iron-enriched cereals with at least 25 percent of the Daily Value for iron to help prevent anemia.*
Note, however, the iron in breakfast cereals is poorly absorbed compared to the iron in lean red meats. But you can enhance iron absorption by drinking a glass of orange juice or enjoying another source of vitamin C (such as grapefruit, cantaloupe, strawberries, or kiwi) along with the cereal. Any iron is better than no iron.

If you tend to eat "all-natural" types of cereals, such as granola and shredded wheat, be aware that these types have "no additives," hence no added iron. You might want to mix and match all-natural brands with iron-enriched brands (or make the effort to eat iron-rich foods at other meals).

2. *Choose fiber-rich bran cereals with more than 5 grams of fiber per serving.*
Fiber not only helps prevent constipation but also is a protective nutrient that may reduce your risk of colon cancer and heart disease. Bran cereals are the best sources of fiber, more so than even fruits and vegetables. Choose from All-Bran, 40% Bran Flakes, Raisin Bran,

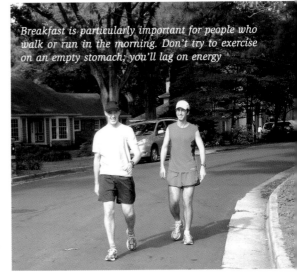

Breakfast is particularly important for people who walk or run in the morning. Don't try to exercise on an empty stomach; you'll lag on energy

Bran Chex, Fiber One or any of the numerous cereals with "bran" or "fiber" in the name. You can also mix high- and low-fiber cereals (Rice Crispies + Fiber One; Special K + Raisin Bran) to boost their fiber value.

Note: If you have trouble with diarrhea when running, you may want to forgo bran cereals. The extra fiber may aggravate the situation.

3. *Choose cereals with whole grains listed among the first ingredients.*
Whole grains include whole wheat, brown rice, corn, and oats; these should be listed first in the ingredients. In my opinion, you should pay more attention to a cereal's grain content than its sugar or sodium (salt) content. Here's why:
- Sodium is a concern primarily for people with high blood pressure. Most runners have low blood pressure and are unlikely to suffer health consequences from choosing cereals with a little added salt. Plus, runners who sweat heavily lose sodium and need to replace it.
- Sugar is simply a carbohydrate that fuels your muscles. Yes, sugar calories are nutritionally empty calories. But when sugar is combined with milk, banana, and the cereal itself, the twenty empty calories in five grams of added sugar are insignificant. Obviously, sugar-filled frosted flakes and kids' cereals with fifteen grams of sugar or more per serving are more like dessert than breakfast. Hence, try to limit your breakfast choices to cereals with fewer than five grams of added sugar per serving. Enjoy the sugary ones for snacks or dessert, if desired, or mix a little with low-sugar cereals.

4. *Choose primarily lowfat cereals with less than two grams of fat per serving.*
High-fat cereals such as some brands of granola and crunchy cookie-type cereals can add unexpected fat and calories to your sports diet. Select lowfat brands for the foundation of your breakfast, and then use only a sprinkling of the higher-fat treats, if desired, for a topping.

Mix 'n Match Cereals
When it comes to cereals, you may not find one that meets all of your standards for whole grain, high fiber, high iron and low fat, but you can always mix-and-match to create a winning combination.

Brand	Iron (%DV)	Fiber (g)	Fat (g)
"Ideal cereal"	>25%	>5	<2
Cheerios, 1 cup (30g)	45%	3	2
Wheaties, 1 cup (30 g)	45%	3	1
Kashi Go Lean, 1 cup (52 g)	10%	10	1
Raisin Bran, Kellogg's. 1 cup (59 g)	25%	7	1.5
Fiber One, 1/2 cup (30 g)	25%	14	1
Quaker 100% Natural, 1/2 cup (48 g)	6%	3	6
Oat Squares, Quaker, 1 cup (60 g)	90%	5	2.5
Cap'n Crunch, 3/4 cup (30 g)	25%	1	1.5

Summary

What you eat in the morning provides fuel for a high-energy day and stronger workouts. Breakfast helps novice and experienced marathoners alike to make their way to the winners' circle! Even dieters can enjoy breakfast without the fear of "getting fat"—that is, breakfast helps curb evening appetite so that dieters can eat lighter at night.

If you generally skip breakfast, at least give breakfast a try during your marathon training. You'll soon learn why breakfast is the meal of champions!

Recipe for Success: Banana Bread

When you are confronted with bananas that are getting too ripe, consider making this recipe for banana bread. You'll enjoy it for a quick but hearty breakfast, lunch, or snack. Add some peanut butter and a glass of lowfat milk for a well-balanced meal and energy for the long run.

3 large bananas, the riper the better
1 egg or 2 egg whites
2 tbsp. (30 g) oil, preferably canola
1/3 to 1/2 cup (70-100 g) sugar
1/4 cup (60 ml) milk
1 tsp. (5 g) salt, as desired
1 tsp. (5 g) baking soda
1/2 tsp. (2.3) baking powder
1 1/2 cups (180 g) flour, preferably half white, half whole-wheat

1. Preheat oven to 350°F (175°C).
2. Spray a 9x5-inch loaf pan with cooking spray.
3. In a large bowl, mash the bananas with a fork.
4. Add the egg, oil, sugar, milk, and salt. Beat well, and then add the baking soda and baking powder.
5. Gently blend the flour into the banana mixture. Stir for 20 seconds or until just moistened.
6. Pour the batter into the prepared pan.
7. Bake at 350°F (175°C) for 45 minutes or until a toothpick inserted near the middle comes out clean.

YIELD: 1 loaf, 12 slices
Total calories: 1,600
Calories per slice: 140

Carbodydrate	24 g
Protein	3 g
Fat	3 g

From: *Nancy Clark's Sport Nutrition Guidebook, Fourth Edition* (Human Kinetics, 2008)

Chapter 3

How to Manage Lunch, Snacks, and Dinner

Whereas breakfast is the most important meal of your training diet, lunch is the second most important meal. In fact, I encourage marathoners to eat TWO lunches! One lunch at 11:00 a.m., when you first start to get hungry, then a second lunch about 3:00 or 4:00 in the afternoon, when the munchies strike. If you train in the morning, these lunches refuel your muscles. If you train in the late afternoon, these lunches prepare you for a strong workout. And in either case, two lunches curb your appetite so you are not starving at the end of the day and have the energy to cook a nutritious dinner.

I invite you to experiment with this two-lunch concept. If you are like most of my clients, you'll find yourself looking forward to a second sandwich to boost your energy at the end of the day. Afraid that two lunches will be fattening? Fear not; a second lunch does not mean additional calories. You'll simply be trading your afternoon cookies and evening ice cream for a wholesome afternoon meal. No longer will you search for evening snacks; you won't be hungry for them.

What's for lunch?

Marathoners commonly have three options for lunch: pack your own, pick up some fast food, or enjoy a hot meal from the cafeteria at work or school. You can eat healthfully in each of these scenarios; just remember to enjoy three kinds of wholesome food with each meal (bread + peanut butter + banana; pizza crust + tomato sauce + cheese; chicken + rice + vegetables) and at least 500 to 600 calories per meal (based on a 2,000 to 2,400 calorie food plan, the amount appropriate for marathoners who want to lose weight; non-dieters can target about 600 to 800 calories per meal).

Eating a hot meal in the middle of the day can make dinnertime easier for marathoners who train in the late afternoon, arrive home starved and don't feel like cooking. By enjoying a nice meal at noon, you'll be content to have a simple supper, such as soup-and-sandwich. For hot meal suggestions, see the section on *Dinner and Marathoners* (page 34).

Pack-your-own lunches

Packing you own lunch is a good way to save money, time, and oftentimes saturated fat and calories if you are organized enough to have the right foods on hand. Good nutrition certainly starts in the supermarket! One trick to packing your lunch is to schedule "food shopping" into your training log. A second trick is to make lunch the night before.

The following suggestions can help you pack a super sports lunch.
- To prevent sandwich bread from getting stale, keep in it the freezer and take out the slices as needed. Bread thaws in minutes at room temperature, or in seconds in the microwave oven.

- Make several sandwiches at one time, and then store them in the freezer. The frozen sandwich will be thawed—and fresh—by lunchtime. Sliced turkey, lean roast beef, peanut butter, and leftover pizza freeze nicely. Don't freeze eggs, mayonnaise, jelly, lettuce, tomatoes, or raw veggies.
- Instead of eating a dry sandwich with no mayonnaise, add moistness using lowfat mayonnaise; lowfat bottled salad dressings, such as ranch or creamy Italian; mustard or ketchup; lettuce and tomato.
- Enjoy peanut butter! It is filled with health-protective fat that reduces your risk of heart disease and diabetes. Combine peanut butter (or other nut butters) with sliced banana, raisins, dates, sunflower seeds, apple slices, and/or celery slices.
- Add zip to a (lowfat) cheese sandwich with oregano, Italian seasonings, green peppers, and/or tomatoes.
- Pack leftover soups, chili, and pasta dinners for the next day's lunch. You can either eat the leftovers cold, or heat them in the office microwave oven.

Fast-Food Lunches

Because of busy schedules, few marathoners make the effort to organize their lunch plans in advance of noontime. Hence, fast foods can save the day—or they can spoil your sports diet. The good news is most quick-service restaurants now offer more lowfat foods than ever before. But, you'll still be confronted by the fatty temptations that jump out at you. Before succumbing to grease, remind yourself that you will feel better and feel better about yourself if you eat well. Here are suggestions for some lower-fat choices:

Dunkin' Donuts: Egg white veggie flatbread, bagel, juice, chicken noodle soup, (decaf) latte light

Deli: Bagel with bean or broth-based soups; sandwiches or subs with whole grain bread and half the filling, little or no mayonnaise (Or, ask for two extra slices of bread or a second roll to make a sandwich for your second lunch with the excessive meat.)

McDonald's: Grilled chicken sandwich, apple dippers, high-carb fluids such as juices, chocolate milk, hot cocoa with nonfat milk, and yes, even soft drinks (in moderation) can fuel your muscles.

Wendy's: Bowl of chili with a plain baked potato

Taco Bell: Bean burrito, Fresco chicken soft taco, Gordita Baja Fresco-style

Pizza: Thick-crust (preferably whole wheat) with extra veggies rather than extra cheese or pepperoni

Pasta: Spaghetti or ziti with tomato sauce and a glass of lowfat milk for protein. Be cautious of lasagna, tortellini, or manicotti that are filled with cheese (i.e., high in saturated fat).

Chinese: Hot and sour or wonton soup; plain rice with stir-fried entrées such as beef and broccoli or chicken with pea pods. Request the food be cooked with minimal oil. Limit fried appetizers and fried entrées.

Salad for Lunch

Salads, whether served as a main dish or an accompaniment, are a simple way to boost your intake of fresh vegetables; that's good! But as a marathoner, you need a substantial, carbohydrate-based lunch; most salads get the bulk of their calories from salad oil; bad! You'll be better able to fuel your muscles if you choose a sandwich with a side salad for lunch, rather then eat just a big salad for the entire meal.

Three tricks to making a healthy sports salad are:

1. Choose a variety of colorful vegetables—dark green lettuces, red tomatoes, yellow peppers, and orange carrots—for a variety of vitamins and minerals.
2. Monitor the dressing. Some marathoners drown 50 calories of healthful salad ingredients with 400 calories of blue cheese dressing!
3. Add extra carbohydrates:
   - dense vegetables, such as corn, peas, beets, carrots
   - beans and legumes, such as chickpeas, kidney beans, and three-bean salad
   - cooked rice or pasta
   - oranges, apples, raisins, grapes, dried cranberries
   - toasted croutons
   - whole-grain bread or roll on the side

Salads

Here are how some popular salad ingredients compare. Note that the ones with the most color have the most nutritional value.

Salad Ingredient	Vitamin C (mg)	Vitamin A (IU)	Magnesium (mg)
Daily Value	60	5,000	400
Broccoli, 5" stalk (180 g)	110	2,500	24
Green pepper, 1/2 (70 g)	65	210	20
Spinach, 2 cups raw (110 g)	50	8,100	90
Tomato, medium (12 g)	25	760	15
Romaine, 2 cups (110 g)	30	3,000	10
Iceburg, 2 cups (110 g)	5	360	5
Cucumber, 1/2 medium (150 g)	10	325	15
Celery, 1 stalk (40 g)	5	55	4

If you choose to use regular dressings, try to select ones made with olive oil for both a nice flavor and health-protective monounsaturated fats. If you want to reduce your fat intake, simply dilute regular dressings with water, more vinegar, or even milk (in ranch and other mayonnaise-based dressings). Or, choose from the plethora of lowfat and fat-free salad dressings. Lowfat dressings are good not only for salads, but also sandwiches, baked potatoes, and dips.

If the vegetables you buy for salads tend to spoil in your refrigerator before you get around to eating them all, buy smaller amounts from a salad bar at the grocery store or deli.

Solving the Four O'clock Munchies Problem

Many marathoners believe eating in the afternoon is sinful. They self-inflict "Thou shalt not snack" as an Eleventh Commandment. Then, they succumb and feel guilty. As I have mentioned before, hunger is simply your body's request for fuel. Hunger is neither bad nor wrong. It is a normal physiological function. You can expect to get hungry every 4 hours. For example, if you eat lunch at noon, you can appropriately be hungry by 4:00. Eat something—preferably a second lunch!

"Second lunch" conjures up visions of real food—a second sandwich, a mug of soup, or peanut butter on crackers and a (decaf) latte. In comparison, "afternoon snack" suggests candy, cookies and sweets. Marathoners who fail to eat enough at breakfast and first lunch generally crave afternoon sweets. The preferred solution to sweet cravings is to prevent the cravings by eating more food earlier in the day.

A second lunch is particularly important for dieters. As I will discuss in Chapter 15, a planned afternoon lunch of 300 to 500 calories (or whatever fits into your calorie budget) will prevent extreme hunger and reduce the risk of blowing your diet that evening.

Second Lunch Suggestions

Some marathoners enjoy a second sandwich for their second lunch. But others like to graze on two or three wholesome snacks from this list. If you carry snacks with you, or keep a supply of "emergency food" in your desk drawer that's ready and waiting for the 4 o'clock munchies, you can avoid the temptations that lurk in every convenience store, vending machine, or bakery. Try to pick items from two or three different food groups, such as carrots + cottage cheese + crackers; or graham crackers + peanut butter + apple.

Perishable snacks to carry with you or buy fresh:	Nonperishable snacks to keep stocked in your desk drawer:
whole wheat bagel	cold cereal (by the handful right out of the box or in a bowl with milk)
lowfat bran muffin	
microwaved potato	hot cereal (packets of instant oatmeal are easy)
Greek yogurt, lowfat	reduced-fat microwave popcorn
cottage cheese, lowfat	canned soup
cheese sticks, lowfat	canned tuna
hard boiled egg	lowfat crackers (Ak-Mak, Wasa, Melba Toast)
hummus and pita bread	graham crackers
thick-crust pizza	granola bars
fresh fruit	energy bars
baby carrots	juice boxes or bottled juice
leftover pasta	dried fruit
frozen meal	peanut butter or other nut butters
peanut butter sandwich	nuts, trail mix

Vending machine snacks: Vending-machine cuisine offers tough choices. But tucked between the lackluster choices, you may be able to find pretzels, peanuts, juice, yogurt, or even an apple. The good part about vending-machine snacks is that they are limited in size (e.g., only three cookies instead of the whole bag) and generally provide only 200 to 400 calories, not 2,000.

If trying to decide between fatty or sugary choices (i.e., chips v. jelly beans), remember that the sugar in jellybeans will at least fuel your muscles, whereas the fat in the chips will clog the arteries. (After eating a sugary snack, be sure to brush or rinse your teeth.)

Cookie Monster snacks: If it's cookies, brownies, an ice cream sundae, or any other such treat that you crave once a week or so, I recommend you satisfy your hankering by enjoying the treat in place of one of your lunches. Simply trade in your lunch-calories for treat-calories, so you won't be overeating. You won't destroy your health with an occasional treat, as long as your overall diet tends to be wholesome. Looking at the weekly picture, you want to target a diet that averages 90% quality foods, 10% treats.

Dinner and Marathoners

Dinnertime generally marks the end of the workday, a time to relax and enjoy a pleasant meal, that is, if you have the energy to prepare it. The trick to dining on a balanced dinner—the protein-starch-vegetable kind that mom used to make with at least three kinds of foods—is to arrive home with enough energy to cook. This means fueling your body and brain with adequate calories prior to dinnertime—with a second lunch.

If you are far from being a master chef, you might want to take a cooking class at your local center for adult education. But no number of cooking classes will help if you arrive home too hungry to cook or make wise food choices.

Quick Fixes: Dinner Tips for Hungry Runners

Because good nutrition starts in the supermarket, you have a far better chance of achieving a super sports diet when your kitchen is well stocked with appropriate foods. You might want to muster up your energy to marathon shop at the discount or warehouse food store once every two or three weeks and really shop, so that you have enough food to last for a while. To help accomplish this goal, post a copy of the sidebar: *Marathoner's Basic Shopping List* on your refrigerator and check off the foods you need.

By keeping your kitchen well stocked with basic foods, you will have the makings for simple meals such as
- Spaghetti with tomato sauce plus hamburger, ground turkey, tofu, beans, cheese cottage, grated cheese, and/or vegetables.

Marathoner's Basic Shopping List
Keep this on our refrigerator and be sure to notice when an item gets low and needs to be replaced.

Cupboard: oatmeal, whole grain cereals, pasta, spaghetti sauce, brown rice, whole grain crackers, baked corn chips, kidney beans, baked beans, refried beans, chickpeas, tuna, canned salmon, peanut butter, soups (mushroom for making casseroles, lentil, minestrone, hearty bean), baking potatoes, V-8 and other vegetable juices

Refrigerator: lowfat Cheddar, mozzarella and cottage cheese, lowfat milk or soymilk, (Greek) yogurt, Parmesan cheese, eggs, tofu, tortillas, baby carrots, lettuce, tomatoes, oranges, bananas (when refrigerated, the banana peel turns black but the fruit itself is fine and lasts longer), fresh fruit in season.

Freezer: whole-grain bagels, pita, English muffins and bread, orange juice concentrate, strawberries, blueberries, broccoli, spinach, winter squash, ground turkey, extra-lean hamburger, chicken (pieces frozen individually in baggies).

- English muffin or pita pizzas
- Tuna noodle casserole
- Soup and sandwiches (tuna, toasted cheese, peanut butter with banana)
- Microwaved potato topped with cottage cheese, baked beans, or yogurt
- Peanut butter crackers and V-8 juice
- Bean burritos (frozen, or made with canned refried beans + salsa + tortilla)

Some runners use their morning shower/shave time to cook 1.5 cups of raw rice while getting ready for work. Come dinnertime, they simply brown one pound of lean hamburger or ground turkey in a large skillet, dump in the cooked rice, and then add whatever is handy. By cooking 1.5 cups or raw rice for each pound of raw lean meat, they generate two generous sports meals with 60 percent of the calories from carbohydrates.

Some popular creations with rice and ground meat include:
- Mexican—add canned beans + chili powder + grated lowfat Cheddar cheese + diced tomatoes
- Chinese—add broccoli zapped in the microwave oven while the meat cooks + soy sauce
- Italian—add green beans + Italian seasonings such as basil, oregano, and garlic powder
- American—add grated lowfat Cheddar cheese + onion browned with the meat + diced tomatoes

Soup and Marathoners

Thick and hearty soups, abundant with carbs from rice, barley, or beans, are welcomed foods for marathoners. The soups' carbs refuel the muscles and the broth replaces the water and sodium lost in sweat. I like to keep soups and stews on hand for quick evening meals that simply need to be heated. A bowl of warm soup is a relatively effortless dinner, thanks to the microwave oven—and a wonderful greeting upon returning from a long winter run!

If you frequently make soups or stews, you might want to:
- Save the cooking water from vegetables in a jar in the refrigerator to use as a soup base.
- Limit the seasonings so that you can add the seasoning-of-the-day into the individual portion you will be eating. That way, you can have Chinese-style chicken soup one day, curried chicken soup another, and Mexican a third.

There is nothing wrong with using canned soups or broths for the foundation of a quick and easy meal. Because the canned products tend to have more sodium than do some homemade soups and stews, runners with high blood pressure should choose the low-sodium canned soups.

Here are some ways to convert plain ol' canned soup into a more exotic meal, light supper, or snack:

- **Combine soups**
  onion and chicken noodle
  tomato and vegetable

- **Add ingredients**
  diced celery, broccoli, tomatoes, or whatever fresh or frozen vegetable is handy
  leftover rice, noodles, pasta
  leftover vegetables, salads, casseroles
  whatever in the 'fridge needs to be eaten

- **Add seasonings**
  curry powder to chicken soup
  cloves to tomato soup
  wine, sherry, vermouth to mushroom soup

- **Add toppings**
  Parmesan cheese
  grated lowfat cheeses
  cottage cheese
  sesame seeds
  croutons

Pasta and Marathoners

Every marathoner regardless of language understands the word pasta. Pasta parties are universally enjoyed around the world. Pasta is popular not only pre-marathon, but also as a standard part of the training diet. Even marathoners who claim they can't cook manage to boil pasta in one shape or another. Some choose to eat pasta at least five nights of the week thinking it is a kind of superfood. Wrong.

Granted, pasta is carbohydrate-rich, quick and easy to cook, heart-healthy, economical, fun to eat, and enjoyed by just about every member of the family. But in terms of vitamins, minerals, and protein, plain pasta is a lackluster food. Here's some information to help you to place pasta in perspective.

Nutritional Value: Pasta is an excellent source of carbohydrates for muscle fuel and is the equivalent of "gas" for your engine. But plain pasta is a marginal source of vitamins and minerals, the "spark plugs" you need for top performance. Pasta is simply made from refined white flour—the same stuff you get in "wonder breads"—with a few vitamins added to replace those lost during processing. Whole-wheat pastas offer a little nutritional boost, but wheat and other grains, in general, are better respected for their carbohydrate-value than their vitamins and minerals. Spinach and tomato pastas also get overrated since they contain relatively little spinach or tomato in comparison to having a serving of that vegetable along with the meal.

Pasta's nutritional value comes from the sauces:
- tomato sauce rich in vitamins A and C and potassium
- pesto-type sauces rich in vitamins A and C and potassium
- clam sauce rich in protein, zinc, and iron.

Be cautious with pasta smothered with butter, cream, or greasy meat sauces. Creamy, cheesy pastas can be artery-clogging nutritional nightmares.

Pasta and Protein: Pasta is popular not only for carbohydrates but also for being a vegetarian alternative to meat-based meals. However, many marathoners live on too much pasta and neglect their protein needs. For example, Joe, an aspiring Olympian, thought his high-carbohydrate, lowfat

Sharing enjoyable meals with your training partners is one of the pleasures of marathoning. Plan ahead!

diet of pasta and tomato sauce seven nights per week was top notch. He came to me wondering why he felt chronically tired and was not improving despite hard training.

The answer was simple. His limited diet was deficient in not only protein but also iron and zinc. Once he started to supplement the pasta with a variety of proteins, he started to feel better, run better, and recover better. He added to his tomato sauce a variety of protein-rich choices:

- extra-lean ground beef or turkey:
- grated lowfat mozzarella cheese
- tofu
- canned, drained kidney beans
- canned tuna
- minced clams
- lowfat cottage cheese

Or, instead of adding protein to the sauce, he drank two glasses of lowfat milk with the meal.

Summary

If you are like many marathoners who struggle with eating well on a daily basis, you need to remember the following keys to a successful sports diet:

1. Eat appropriately sized meals at least every four hours (such as 7:00 a.m.-11:00-3:00-7:00 p.m.) so that you won't get too hungry. Notice how your lunches and dinner deteriorate when you eat too little breakfast and get too hungry.

2. Spend your calories on a variety of wholesome foods at each meal; target at least three kinds of food per meal.

3. Pay attention to how much better you feel, run, and feel about yourself when you eat a well balanced sports diet.

It's my opinion that getting too hungry is the biggest problem with most marathoners' diets. Hearty meals based on carb-rich whole grains, fruit and vegetables set the stage for a top-notch sports diet.

Sweet Potato Fries

Sweet potato fries are yummy for dinner or even a snack. They offer a healthful way to satisfy your sweet tooth while fueling your muscles with vitamin-rich carbs.

2 medium (1 pound; 0.5 kg) sweet potatoes or yams
2 tablespoons (30 g) oil, preferably olive or canola
2 tablespoons (25 g) brown sugar

1. Wash and thinly slice sweet potatoes into coin shapes.
2. Mix olive oil and brown sugar in a bowl. Add the sweet potatoes and mix well to coat the "coins."
3. Place them on a baking sheet lined with foil (for easy clean-up).
4. Bake at 425° F (220° C) degrees for about 25 to 35 minutes, or until tender. Flip them half-way through baking.

Yield: 3 servings
Total Calories: 750
Calories per serving: 250

42 g Carbohydrate
2 g Protein
8 g Fat

Recipe courtesy of Cat Whitehill. Reprinted with permission from *Food Guide for Soccer: Tips and Recipes From the Pros* by Gloria Averbuch and Nancy Clark.

Chapter 4

Vitamins and Supplements for Marathoners

More than half of Americans take dietary supplements in the belief that they will make them feel better, give them greater energy, improve their health, and prevent and treat disease. Users spend more than $23 billion a year on dietary supplements; the vitamin industry is a booming business.

> **Vitamin pills are great, but there's no substitute for the real thing.**
>
> *Jonathan Dietrich, Washington, DC*

Vitamins are essential substances that your body can't make. They perform important jobs in your body, including helping to convert food into energy. (Vitamins do *not* provide energy, however; carbohydrates do.) Although a supplement is certainly a quick and easy safety net for hit-or-miss eating, I highly recommend that you first make the effort to "eat" your vitamins via natural foods. As a hungry marathoner who requires more calories than the average person, you can easily consume large doses of vitamins in, let's say, a taller glass of orange juice or bigger pile of steamed broccoli. Chapter 1 has information about some of the best food sources of vitamins.

Because food consumption surveys suggest that many people fail to eat a well-balanced variety of wholesome foods, some runners and walkers may indeed suffer from marginal nutritional deficiencies, particularly those who:
- restrict calories
- eat a repetitive diet of rice cakes and apples
- skimp on fruits, vegetables, and dairy foods
- over-indulge in fats and sweets.

Even marathoners who believe they eat well sometimes miss the mark. For example, one woman who took pride in her high-carbohydrate, lowfat diet (primarily bagels, bananas, pasta, and pretzels) ate too many carbohydrates at the exclusion of other foods (such as meats and dairy). She had a diet deficient in calcium, iron, zinc, and protein.

As a result of American's unbalanced food choices, should the general public be encouraged to take a supplement to compensate for poor eating habits? Not necessarily. Despite the rising popularity of supplements, many health organizations, including the American Heart Association and the National Institutes of Health, recommend food, not pills, for optimal nutrition. That's because food contains far more than just vitamins. It contains phytochemicals, fiber and other health-protective substances that are not in pills. Hence, the key to good health is to learn how to eat well despite a hectic lifestyle.

Let's take a look at some of what is and what is not known about nutritional supplements, and hopefully you'll see why spending more money on broccoli and orange juice rather than on pills and potions is the wiser bet. Whole foods offer protein, carbohydrates, fiber, and phytochemicals—far more than just vitamins and minerals.

Vitamins were originally studied to determine the minimal amount of a nutrient required to prevent deficiency diseases such as beriberi and scurvy. The recommended dietary allowances were developed to guide people towards an appropriate intake; they include a large safety margin. For example, in the US, the Dietary Reference Intake (DRI) for vitamin C is 75 to 90 milligrams (women, men); this is four times the minimal amount needed to prevent the deficiency disease scurvy. The question remains unanswered: What is the optimal level of vitamins, not just to prevent deficiency, but also to enhance health?

No amount of any supplement will compensate for a high-fat, hit-or-miss diet and stress-filled lifestyle. But supplements are indeed appropriate for certain populations, including:
- folic acid for pregnant women and women who might become pregnant (expectedly or unexpectedly), to prevent certain birth defects
- iron for vegetarians and women with heavy menstrual periods
- zinc and anti-oxidants for nonsmokers with macular degeneration (an eye disease)
- vitamin D and calcium for postmenopausal women for strong bones
- vitamin D for people who live in northern latitudes.

To date, no studies have documented a physiological need for mega-doses of vitamins, even for marathoners and other athletes. Most athletes can consume more than enough vitamins through their daily food intake.

Marathoners who eat vitamin-enriched energy bars and breakfast cereals, as well as other enriched grain foods, commonly consume far more vitamins than they realize. But take note: runners who eat primarily "all natural foods" from the whole foods stores miss out on the benefit of enriched foods. ("All natural foods" have no added vitamins or minerals, like iron.). That's one reason why the government acknowledges that some of our grains can appropriately come from enriched foods.

Food Offers More Than Vitamins

Whole foods such as fruits and vegetables offer hundreds, perhaps thousands, of substances called *phytochemicals* that protect our health. These include:
- *protease inhibitors* in soybeans that may slow tumor growth
- *isoflavones* in dried beans that may reduce the risk of breast or ovarian cancer
- *isothiocyanates* in broccoli that may help block carcinogens from damaging a cell's DNA

These phytochemicals may explain why the cruciferous vegetables such as broccoli, cabbage, and cauliflower are thought to be protective against cancer, and onions and garlic are thought to be protective against heart disease. Deeply colored, antioxidant-rich fruits such as tart cherries, blueberries, grape juice and pomegranate juice can enhance your health and recovery from exercise. Yet, taking high doses of anti-oxidant supplements such as vitamins C and E may create an imbalance that has a negative effect on your immune system.

While not a vitamin, omega-3 fish oil is another nutrient found in food that is powerfully health protective. The American Heart Association recommends that healthy people eat 12 ounces (two to three servings) of preferably oily fish, such as salmon and tuna, each week to provide the omega-3 fats that protect against heart disease. For non-fish eaters, flaxseed, walnuts, and canola oil can be plant-based alternatives. Take heed: even fit marathoners are not immune from heart disease!

As you decide your nutritional fate, know that a diet based on a variety of wholesome foods is your best source of good nutrition. If you choose to take a supplement for its potential health-protective effects, be sure to do so in *addition to eating well*. Because researchers have yet to unravel the whole vitamin/health mystery, stay tuned and be sure to take care of your whole health. The phytochemicals, omega-3 fats and other unknown substances found in whole foods, but not in pills, tend to emerge as the winner.

Am I sick? Am I tired? Do I Need Vitamins?

Exercise energizes many people, enhancing their productivity as well as relieving their stress. But some marathoners complain of chronic fatigue. They feel run down, dragged out, and overwhelmingly exhausted. If this sounds familiar, you may wonder if you are sick, overtired, or if something is wrong with your diet. You may wonder if taking vitamins would solve the problem.

Perhaps you can relate to Peter, a 39-year-old marathon runner, lawyer, and solo-chef who bemoaned, "I just don't take the time to eat right. My diet is awful. I rarely eat fruits or vegetables, to say nothing of a real meal. I think that poor nutrition is catching up with me. What vitamins should I take?"

Peter lived alone, hated to cook for just himself, tended to survive on fast (and fatty) foods. He rarely ate breakfast, barely ate lunch, but always collapsed after a long day with a generous feast of a large deli sandwich, Chinese take-out, or pizza. He struggled to wake up in the morning, to stay awake during afternoon meetings, and to grind through his daily ten-mile run.

I evaluated Peter's diet, calculated that he required about 3,000 calories per day (700 to 800 calories per meal—breakfast, lunch #1, lunch #2, dinner), and suggested a few simple food changes that could result in higher energy, greater stamina, and better running. Trying to find some solutions to Peter's fatigue, I explored the following questions. Perhaps the answers will offer solutions for your energy problems.

- *Are you tired due to low blood sugar?* Peter skipped not only breakfast but also often missed lunch because he "didn't have time." He would doze off in the afternoon because he had low blood sugar. With zero calories to feed his brain, he ended up feeling sleepy.

The solution was to choose to make time to eat. Just as he chose to sleep later in the morning, he could choose to stock trail mix (granola, nuts, and raisins) at the office, so he could munch on that for his morning fuel. He could also choose to stop working for five or ten minutes to eat lunch.

- *Is your diet too low in carbohydrates?* Peter's fast-but-fatty food choices filled his stomach but left his muscles poorly fueled with inadequate glycogen to support his training program. Higher carbohydrate snacks and meals would not only would fuel his muscles but also help maintain a normal blood sugar level thereby providing energy for mental work as well as physical exercise.

- *Are you iron-deficient and anemic?* Peter ate little red meat and consequently little iron, an important mineral in red blood cells that helps carry oxygen to exercising muscles. Iron-deficiency anemia can result in needless fatigue during exercise. I taught Peter how to boost his dietary iron intake, with or without meat. (See chapter 6.) I also recommended he talk to his doctor about getting his blood tested (hemoglobin, hematocrit, ferritin, serum iron, and total iron-binding capacity) to rule out the question of anemia.

- *Are you getting enough sleep?* Peter's complaint about being chronically tired was justified because he was tired both mentally (from his intense job) and physically (from his strenuous training). He worked from 8 a.m. to 8 p.m. By the time he got home, ran, ate dinner, and "unwound," midnight had rolled around. The wake-up bell at 6:30 a.m. came all too soon—especially since Peter often had trouble falling asleep due to having eaten such a large dinner.
  I recommended that Peter try to get more sleep by eating lighter dinners (soup and sandwich, or even cereal), having bigger breakfasts, and scheduling his main meal at noon (lowfat Chinese meals, vegetable soup and hearty sandwich, or pasta). By trading in 1,200 of his evening calories for 600 more calories at breakfast and 600 more calories at lunch, he could determine if less food in his stomach before bed would result in better sleep.

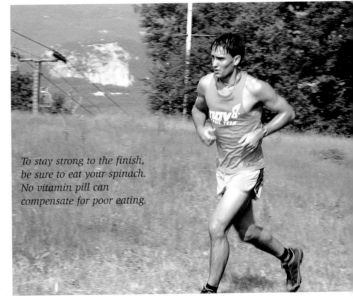

To stay strong to the finish, be sure to eat your spinach. No vitamin pill can compensate for poor eating.

- *Are you overtraining?* Although Peter took pride in the fact that he hadn't missed a day of running in seven years, he felt discouraged he wasn't improving despite harder training. I questioned whether he was a "compulsive runner" who punished his body or a "serious athlete" who trained wisely and took rest days. One or two rest days or easy days per week are an essential part of a training program; they allow the muscles to heal and to replenish their depleted glycogen stores.

- *Are you stressed or depressed?* Peter not only had a stressful job, he was also dealing with the stress and depression associated with family problems, to say nothing of the challenges of training for a marathon. Since he was feeling a bit helpless with this situation, I encouraged him to successfully control at least one aspect of his life—his diet. Simple dietary improvements would help him feel better not only physically but also mentally. This would be very energizing in itself.

If you answered "yes" to many of the questions I asked Peter, you may be able to resolve your fatigue with better eating, sleeping, and training habits—not with vitamin pills. Experiment with the simple food suggestions in this book. Before long you may transform your current low-energy patterns into a food plan for success! Eating well is not as hard as you may think.

Summary

Your best bet for fighting fatigue is to be responsible with your food choices and nourish your body with the right balance of wholesome foods. Make the effort to eat a variety of foods and fluids from the different food groups every day. Eating marathoner's portions, you will consume not only the amounts of the vitamins and minerals you need, you will also be giving your body the calories it needs to prevent fatigue.

If you are tempted to take supplements for health insurance, do so only if you simultaneously choose to eat a healthful diet. Remember, no amount of supplements will compensate for an inadequate diet—but you will always win with good nutrition. Eat wisely, eat well!

For more information
Confusion abounds regarding dietary supplements, their safety, and their potential health benefits. Here are some websites that offer abundant information about vitamins and health. (You might need to do a search on "vitamins" or "fish oil" to find your topic of interest) within each website:

The American Heart Association: **www.americanheart.org**
FDA's Center for Food Safety and Applied Nutrition **www.cfsan.fda.gov**
National Library of Medicine: **www.nlm.nih.gov/medlineplus**
The World's Healthiest Foods: **www.whfoods.org**

A Super Salad

A colorful salad is a super way to boost your nutrient intake! Here's a suggestion for a super salad that is rich in not only vitamins, but also protein (to build muscles), carbs (to fuel muscles), fiber (to move food through your system) and healthful fats and phytochemicals to help fight inflammation.

By eating a portfolio of nutrient-dense foods at most meals, you need not rely on vitamin pills to compensate for lousy eating.

In a large bowl, combine your choice of colorful salad vegetables, such as:
Spinach
Tomato
Red pepper
Yellow pepper
Carrot

Add protein and healthful fat:
Flaked Tuna
Tofu cubes
Chickpeas
Kidney beans
Cottage cheese, lowfat
Shredded cheese, lowfat
Walnuts or almonds, chopped
Avocado slices
Olive oil-based salad dressing

Accompany with your choice of wholesome carbs:
Whole wheat English muffin
Toasted whole grain bread
Fresh rolls
Whole grain crackers

Chapter 5

Carbohydrate Confusion

Carbohydrates are how plants store energy. Hence, all plant foods–fruits, vegetables and grains–are carbohydrate-rich. As a marathoner, you need carbohydrates to fuel your muscles and feed your brain. You can consume carbs by eating bananas, (brown) rice, (whole wheat) pasta, potato, honey, sports drinks, and gumdrops, even marshmallows. Obviously, you'll enhance your health if you choose nutrient-dense carbs primarily from fruits, vegetables, and whole grains. But the sugary foods do offer the "gas" that fuels your muscles. The sugars just fail to offer any health protective vitamins or minerals.

While carb-bashers have long-established sugar as a dietary demon, starches have also gotten a bad rap thanks to Dr. Atkins and his high protein diet. Some marathoners, who had been happily enjoying bagels, pasta and crackers as the foundation of their sports diet, are shunning these excellent sources of muscle fuel. Instead, they choose egg whites, cottage cheese, soy shakes and protein-based foods. They also experience needless fatigue due to poorly fueled muscles.

Today, questions abound about the role of carbohydrates in the sports diet—as well as concerns about insulin (the hormone that helps carbs get stored in the muscles) and the glycemic effect of foods (that is, the rate a carbohydrate enters the blood stream). The purpose of this chapter is to address carbohydrate confusion and provide some clarity for marathoners who want to eat wisely for good health, high energy, weight control, and top performance.

Q: Are carbs fattening? Should I eat less of them?
A. Carbohydrates are not inherently fattening. Excess calories are fattening.
Excess calories of carbohydrates (bread, bagels, pasta) are actually less fattening than are excess calories of fat (butter, mayonnaise, frying oils) because the body has to spend calories to convert excess carbohydrates into body fat. In comparison, the body easily converts excess calories of dietary fat into body fat. This means, if you are destined to be gluttonous but want to suffer the least weight gain, you might want to indulge in (high carb) frozen yogurt instead of (high fat) gourmet ice cream. See Chapter 15 for more information about how to lose weight with a carb-based sports diet.

Q. If carbs aren't fattening, why do high protein diets "work"?
A. High protein diets seemingly "work" because—
1. The dieter loses water weight. Carbs hold water in the muscles. For each ounce of carbohydrate you stored as glycogen, your body simultaneously stores about three ounces of water. When you deplete carbs during exercise, your body releases the water and you experience a significant loss of weight that's mostly water, not fat.
2. People eliminate calories when they eliminate carbohydrates. For example, you might eliminate not only the baked potato (200 calories) but also two pats of butter (100 calories) on top of the potato—and this creates a calorie deficit.
3. Protein tends to be more satiating than is carbohydrate. That is, protein (and fat) lingers longer in the stomach than does carbohydrate. Hence, having 200

calories of high protein eggs for breakfast will satiate you longer than 200 calories of high carb bagel with jam. By curbing hunger, you have fewer urges to eat and can more easily restrict calories—that is, until you start to crave carbs and over-eat them. (You know the scene: "Last chance to eat bagels before I go back on my diet, so I'd better eat them all now...")

The overwhelming reason why high protein diets do NOT work is people fail to stay on them forever. Remember: You should never start a food program you do not want to maintain for the rest of your life. Do you really want to never eat breads, potato or crackers ever again? Your better option is to learn how to manage carbs, not avoid them.

Q. Is there a difference between the carbs from starchy foods (like breads) vs. the carbs in fruits and vegetables or in candy?

A. *As far as your muscles are concerned, there is no difference. You can carbo-load on jellybeans, bananas or brown rice; they are biochemically similar.*
Sugars and starches both offer the same amount of energy (4 calories per gram, or 16 calories per teaspoon) and both can get stored as glycogen in muscles or used for fuel by the brain (via the blood sugar).
The sugar in jellybeans is a simple compound, one or two molecules linked together. The starch in (brown) rice is a complex compound with hundreds to thousands of sugar molecules linked together. Sugars can convert into starches and starches can convert into sugars. For example—
- When a banana is green (not ripe), it is starchy. As it gets older, it becomes sweeter; in fruits, the starch converts into sugar.
- When peas are young, they are sweet. As they get older, they get starchier; in vegetables, the sugar converts into starch.

Grain foods (wheat, rice, corn, oats) also store their energy as complex strands of sugar molecules, a starch. The starch breaks down into individual sugar molecules (glucose) during digestion. Hence, your muscles don't care if you eat sugars or starches for fuel because they both digest into the same simple sugar: glucose.

The difference between sugars and starches comes in their nutritional value and impact on your health. Some sugars and starches are healthier than others. For example, the sugar is orange juice is accompanied by vitamin C, folate and potassium. The sugar in orange soda pop is void of vitamins and minerals; that's why it's described as "empty calories." The starch in whole wheat bread is accompanied by fiber and phytochemicals. The starch in white breads has lost many health protective nutrients during the refining process.

Q. I've heard white bread is "poison." Do you agree?

A. *White bread offers lackluster nutrition, but it is not "poison" nor a "bad" food.*
White bread can be balanced into an overall wholesome diet (as can pasta and other foods made from refined while flour). That is, if you have whole grain Wheaties for breakfast and brown rice for dinner, your diet can accommodate a

sandwich made on white bread for lunch. White breads and food made from refined flour tend to be enriched with B-vitamins, iron and folate—all important nutrients for marathoners. According to the US Dietary Guidelines, about half your grains can appropriately come from whole grains.

Q. Is sugar "evil"?
A. Sugar is fuel, not evil.
While the sugar in oranges and other fruits is accompanied by important vitamins and minerals, the sugar in, let's say, jelly beans, is void of nutritional value. In general, I suggest marathoners limit their refined sugar intake to about 10% of total calories. That's about 200 to 300 calories of sugar per day; 200 calories equates to a quart of Gatorade, two gels, 16 ounces of soda pop, or 10 jellybeans.

Most marathoners can handle sugar just fine. But for a few marathoners, sugar seems "evil" because it contributes to swings in blood sugar levels that can result in feeling lightheaded and shaky. If you are "sugar sensitive" and notice that sugar makes you feel poorly, choose sugar along with protein, such as jelly with peanut butter, apple with lowfat cheese, or fruit yogurt with almonds.

Q. Should I avoid sugar pre-exercise?
A. The best advice regarding pre-exercise sugar is for you to avoid the desire for sugar by having eaten appropriately prior to exercise.
For example, if you crave sugar before an afternoon training run, you could have prevented the desire for sugary, quick-energy foods by having eaten a bigger breakfast and lunch. Sugar cravings can be a sign you have gotten too hungry.
Note that sugar taken during exercise is unlikely to contribute to a hypoglycemic reaction because muscles quickly use the sugar without the need for extra insulin. This includes sports drinks, gels, sports beans, gummy candies and other popular sugary choices. See chapter 10 for more advice about pre-exercise fueling.

Q. Should I choose foods based on their glycemic effect (that is, the rate at which they cause blood sugar to increase)?
A. No. The glycolic response to a food varies from person to person, as well as from meal to meal (depending on the combinations of foods you eat).
You'll be better off experimenting with a variety of grains, fruits and vegetables to learn what food combinations settle well, satisfy your appetite and offer lasting energy. Wholesome, fiber-rich fruits, vegetables, beans and whole grains are wise food choices for active people not because they tend to have a low glycemic effect (that is, cause a slow rise in blood sugar) but because they are nutrient-dense, can curb your appetite, and may even help with weight management.

Summary

As a marathoner (and as a health-conscious person), you should eat carbohydrates as the foundation of each meal. This can mean cereal for breakfast, sandwiches made on hearty bread for lunch, and for dinner, a meal that includes a starch such as whole wheat pasta, sweet potato, or brown rice. While you can also get some carbs from fruits and veggies, most marathoners do not get enough carbs from these foods alone.

Despite popular belief, carbs are not fattening, but rather the preferred source of fuel for your muscles. By fueling and refueling with carb-based meals every day, your muscles will have the energy they need to support your training program. By training at your best, you will be able to complete the marathon at your best.

Pasta, Rice and Potato: Cooking Tips

Here's some information to help you optimize your intake of these super-fuels that should be the foundation of your dinners, especially before long runs.

Pasta

Marathoners around the globe enjoy fueling their muscles with a variety of pasta meals. You can choose from at least 26 shapes of pasta, ranging from angel hair to ziti. All the shapes are made from the same dough; some are tinted with vegetable juice (e.g. spinach, tomato). And all are easy to cook.

Tips for Cooking Pasta

- When trying to decide which shape of pasta to use for a meal, the rule of thumb is to use twisted and curved shapes (such as twists and shells) with meaty, beany, and chunky sauces. The shape will trap more sauce than would the straight strands of spaghetti or linguini.

Here are some quick and easy ideas for pasta toppings:
- Salsa
- Salsa heated in the microwave, then mixed with cottage cheese
- Olive oil with red pepper flakes
- (lowfat) Italian salad dressing mixed with a little Dijon mustard
- (lowfat) salad dressings of your choice with steamed vegetables
- (lowfat) sour cream and Italian seasonings
- Steamed, chopped broccoli with Parmesan cheese
- Parmesan cheese and a sprinkling of herbs (basil, oregano, Italian seasonings)
- Chicken breast sautéed with oil, garlic, onion, and basil
- Chili with kidney beans (and cheese)
- Lentil soup (thick)
- Spaghetti sauce with a spoonful of grape jelly (adds a "sweet 'n sour" taste)
- Spaghetti sauce with canned chicken or tuna, tofu cubes, canned beans, cottage cheese, ground beef or turkey (for protein)

- If you want a quick cooking pasta, choose angel hair, alphabets, and the little stars (stelline).
- To reduce cooking time, you can cook the pasta in half the amount of water (takes half as long to bring to a boil).
- Pasta is done when it starts to look opaque and is tender, yet firm to the teeth; "al dente" as the Italians say.
- When done, drain the pasta into a colander set in the sink. Shake briefly to remove excess water, and then return it to the cooking pot or to a warmed serving bowl. To prevent the pasta from sticking together as it cools, toss the pasta with a little olive or canola oil or tomato sauce.

Rice

Not all runners carbo-load on pasta. Rice is a fine alternative, preferably brown rice that retains the fiber-rich bran. Some marathoners enjoy rice for breakfast, as an alternative to oatmeal.

Tips for Cooking Rice
- Because of its tough bran coat and germ, brown rice needs about 45 to 50 minutes to cook; white rice only about 20 to 30 minutes.
- Consider cooking rice in the morning while you are getting ready for work, so that it will be waiting to be simply reheated when you get home.
- One-half cup of uncooked white or brown rice expands into about 1.5 cups of cooked rice. This is a reasonable portion (350 calories) for a hungry marathoner.
- When cooking rice, cook double amounts for leftovers that you can either freeze or refrigerate.

You can cook rice in a variety of ways. Here are two popular methods:

Boiled rice #1
Bring a saucepan of water to a full boil.

Stir in 1/3 to 1/2 cup of rice per person plus a teaspoon of salt, as desired.

Simmer about 20 minutes, or until a grain of rice is tender when you bite into it.

Drain into a colander, rinse it under hot tap water to remove the sticky starch, and put it back into the saucepan.

Keep the rice warm over low heat, fluffing it with a fork.

Here are a few rice suggestions for hungry marathoners:

Cook rice in—
- Chicken or beef broth
- Mixture of orange or apple juice and water
- Water with seasonings: cinnamon, soy sauce, oregano, curry, chili powder, or whatever might nicely blend with the menu.

Top rice with—
- Leftover chili
- Lowfat or fat-free Italian dressing and mustard
- Toasted sesame seeds
- Steamed vegetables
- Chopped mushrooms and green peppers, either raw or sautéed
- Lowfat or fat-free sour cream, raisins, tuna, and curry powder
- Raisins, cinnamon, and applesauce

Boiled rice #2 (This method retains more of the vitamins that otherwise get lost into the cooking water.)

For each one cup of rice, put two cups of water into a saucepan, and a teaspoon salt, as desired.

Bring to a boil, then cover and turn the heat down low.

Let the rice cook undisturbed until it is tender and all the water has been absorbed.

Stir gently with a fork. Do not over-stir or you'll end up with a gluey mess.

Potatoes

Potatoes are a nutritious source of carbohydrates, more so than plain pasta or rice. A large baking potato offers more than half the vitamin C you need for the day, plus all the potassium you'd lose in three hours of sweaty exercise. A sweet potato offers even more health benefits.

Some marathoners enjoy baked potatoes for not only meals but also snacks. Pre-baked, you can eat them as you might eat a piece of fruit before or after workouts. The standard "restaurant size" potato generally has about 200 calories, similar to an energy bar. Salted boiled potatoes while biking are a popular choice with triathletes.

Here are some tips for enjoying potatoes in your sports diet.

- Potatoes come in different varieties, with some varieties best suited for baking (russets), others for boiling (red or white rounds). Ask the produce manager at your grocery store for guidance.
- Potatoes are best stored in a cool place that is well ventilated, such as your cellar. Do not refrigerate potatoes because they will become sweet and off-colored.
- Rather than peel the skin (a good source of fiber), scrub the skin well, cook it, and eat it, skin and all. Even mashed potatoes can be made unpeeled!
- To bake a potato in the oven, allow about 40 minutes at 400°F (200°C) for a medium potato, closer to an hour for a large potato. Because potatoes can be baked at any temperature, you can simply adjust the cooking time to whatever else is in the oven.

Here are some quick and easy ideas for potato toppings:

- (Lowfat) salad dressing
- (Lowfat) sour cream, chopped onion, and grated lowfat cheddar cheese
- Cottage cheese and garlic powder
- Cottage cheese and salsa
- Milk mashed into the potato
- Plain yogurt
- Mustard or ketchup
- Mustard and Worcestershire sauce
- Vinegar and flavored vinegars
- Soy sauce
- Pesto
- Chopped chives and green onion
- Herbs, such as dill, parsley, chopped chives
- Steamed broccoli or other cooked vegetables
- Chopped jalapeno peppers
- Lentils or lentil soup
- Soup broth
- Applesauce

- The potato is baked enough when you can easily pierce it with a fork.
- To cook a potato in the microwave oven, cut a slit in the top of the potato (to allow the steam to escape, so the potato will be "drier," place it on some paper towels in the microwave, and zap it for about 4 minutes if it is medium-sized, 6 to 10 minutes if large. (Cooking time will vary according to the size of the potato, the power of your oven, and the number of potatoes being cooked.) Turn the potato over halfway through cooking. Remove the potato from the oven, wrap it in a towel and allow it to finish cooking for about 3 to 5 minutes.

Hummus

Hummus is made with chickpeas (garbanzo beans)—an excellent source of not only carbs but also a good source of protein. Enjoy hummus as:
- a dip with pita bread or baby carrots
- a sandwich spread along with turkey
- a roll-up with shredded veggies

The secret ingredient in hummus is tahini—sesame paste. You can buy tahini in the ethnic food section of supermarkets or whole food stores. (Hint: Enjoy the leftover tahini on pasta!)

- 1 16-ounce (480 g) can chickpeas
- 1 tablespoon (15 ml) lemon juice
- 1 clove garlic (or 1/4 tsp/1 g garlic powder) to taste
- 2 tablespoons (30 g) tahini (or peanut butter can be substituted)
- salt and pepper, as desired

Optional: dash of cayenne; 1 tablespoon parsley; 1/2 teaspoon cumin

- Drain the chickpeas, saving 1/4 cup (60 ml) of the liquid.
- In a blender or food processor, mix the chickpeas, 1/4 cup (60 ml) liquid, lemon juice, garlic, tahini, and seasonings.
- Blend until smooth. If you don't have a blender, mash the chickpeas with the back of a fork.
- Serve with pita bread or as a dip for raw vegetables.

Total calories: 625		Carbohydrate	11 g
8 servings		Protein	3 g
One serving: 80 calories		Fat	3 g

RECIPE

Protein for
Marathoners

Due to the influence of protein supplement advertisements, as well as high protein diets (that wrongly deem carbohydrates as fattening), many marathoners have made protein the foundation of their sports diets. They believe a strong protein intake will boost their power and strength, so they eat protein bars or shakes before their long training runs. Wrong choice! Carbs are the preferred source of fuel for muscles. Lean sources of protein should be the accompaniment to a carbohydrate-based sports diet.

Your body needs protein to:

- build and repair muscles
- make red blood cells
- make enzymes and hormones
- grow hair and fingernails

About 10 to 15 percent of your calories should come from protein; that translates into a little bit of protein at each meal. Some marathoners eat more than that; others eat less. Here are some tips to consuming the right amount of protein to optimize performance and recovery.

How Much Protein Is Enough?

The current recommended daily allowance (RDA) for protein is 0.4 grams of protein per pound of body weight (0.8 g/kg). This RDA was based on sedentary college students. Because marathoners have a slightly higher protein need, an adequate and safe protein intake is about 0.5 to 0.8 grams of protein per pound of body weight (1.0 to 1.6 g/kg). Growing teenagers, athletes building new muscles, marathoners doing lots of long runs, or dieters who restrict calories (which results in protein being used for fueling rather than maintaining muscles), should target the higher end of the protein range.

> Be sure to include enough protein in your training diet! I used to eat too many carbs and too little protein, and my performance suffered. Now I make sure to include some chicken or fish with my salads for dinner, and dairy with my breakfast each day. Once I started to pay attention to my protein intake, my recovery after long runs improved dramatically.
>
> *Kip Parker, Atlanta, GA*

How Little Protein is Too Little?

Some marathoners, being health conscious, have reduced their meat (and saturated fat) intake, with hopes of reducing their risk of heart disease. While reducing fatty meat intake is a good idea, some of these non-meat eaters have totally cut out animal proteins; they call themselves "vegetarians" when they are really just "non-meat eaters" because they have failed to add any plant proteins to their daily meals. They live on fruit, vegetables, and pasta. The result is a protein-deficient diet.

If you aspire to a vegetarian diet and have stopped eating animal meats, make sure you are addressing your overall protein needs. You should consume a small amount of protein-containing food (milk, peanut butter, hummus, etc.) at each

How to Balance Your Protein Intake

If you wonder if you are eating too little (or too much) protein, you can estimate your daily protein needs by multiplying your weight (or a good weight for your body) by 0.5 to 0.75 grams of protein per pound (1.0 to 1.6 g Pro/kg).

Weight in lbs (kg)	Protein (grams/day)
100 (45)	50-80
120 (55)	60-90
150 (68)	75-100
170 (77)	85-115

Use food labels and the following chart to calculate your protein intake. Pay close attention to portion sizes!

Approximate Protein Content of Some Commonly Eaten Foods

Animal Proteins	Protein (grams)
Beef, 4 oz, (120g) cooked*	32
Chicken breast, small 4 oz. cooked	32
Tuna, 1 can (6.5 ounces)	35-40
Meat, fish, poultry, 1 oz. (30 g) cooked	7-8
Egg, 1	7
Egg white, 1	3

*4 ounces cooked = size of deck of cards
4 ounces cooked = 5 to 6 ounces raw

Plant Proteins	
Lentils, beans, 1/2 cup (100 g)	7
Baked beans, 1/2 cup (130 g)	7
Peanut butter, 2 tablespoons (30 g)	8
Tofu, 1/4 cake firm (4 oz, 120 g)	8
Soy milk, 1 cup (240 ml)	7

Dairy Products	
Milk, yogurt, 1 cup (240 ml)	8
Greek yogurt, 6-oz tub	14
Cheese, 1 ounce (30 g)	8
Cheese, 1 slice American (2/3 oz; 20 g)	6
Cottage cheese, 1/3 cup (75 g)	8
Milk powder, 1/4 cup (30 g)	8

Breads, Cereals, Grains	
Bread, 1 slice (30 g)	2
Cold cereal, 1 ounce (30 g)	2
Oatmeal, 1/3 cup dry (30 g), or 1 cup cooked	5
Rice, 1/3 cup dry (55 g), or 1 cup cooked	4
Pasta, 2 ounces dry (60 g), or 1 cup cooked	7

Starchy Vegetables	
Peas, carrots, 1/2 cup (80 g) cooked	2
Corn, 1/2 cup cooked (80 g)	2
Beets, 1/2 cup cooked (80 g)	2
Winter squash, 1/2 cup (100 g)	2
Potato, 1 small (125 g)	2

Fruits, Watery Vegetables

Negligible amounts of protein.
Most fruits and vegetables have only small amounts of protein. They may contribute a total of 5 to 10 grams protein per day, depending on how much of them you eat.

Quick and Easy Meatless Meals

Here a few ideas to help you with a meat-free diet that has adequate protein.

Breakfast:
- Cold cereal (preferably iron-enriched, as noted on the label): Top with (soy) milk or (Greek) yogurt and sprinkle with a few nuts.
- Oatmeal, oat bran, and other hot cereals: Add peanut butter, almonds or other nuts, and/or powdered milk.
- Toast, bagels: Top with lowfat cheese, cottage or ricotta cheese, or peanut butter.

Snacks:
- Assorted nuts
- Peanut butter on rice cakes or crackers
- Yogurt (Note: Frozen yogurt has only 4 grams of protein per cup, as compared to 8 grams in regular yogurt, 14 grams in Greek yogurt.)

Lunch and Dinner:
- Salads: Add tofu, chickpeas, three-bean salad, marinated kidney beans, cottage cheese, sunflower seeds, chopped nuts.
- Protein-rich salad dressing: Add salad seasonings to plain yogurt, blenderized tofu or cottage cheese (dilute with milk or yogurt).
- Spaghetti sauce: Add diced tofu and/or canned, drained kidney beans.
- Pasta: Choose protein-enriched pastas that offer 13 grams of protein per cup (140 g), as compared to 8 grams in regular pasta. Top with grated part-skim mozzarella cheese.
- Potato: Bake or microwave, then top with canned beans, baked beans, or lowfat cottage or ricotta cheese.
- Hearty soups: Choose lentil, split pea, bean, and minestrone.
- Hummus: Try hummus with pita or tortillas.
- Cheese pizza: A protein-rich fast food, half of a 12-inch pizza has about 40 grams of protein.

meal. Otherwise, you'll feel the results of a protein imbalance: chronic fatigue, anemia, lack of improvement, muscle wasting, and an overall run-down feeling.

Marathoners with big appetites can more easily consume adequate protein than can calorie-conscious dieters. That is, if you eat only a smidgen of peanut butter on a lunchtime sandwich and a sprinkling of garbanzo beans on a dinner salad, you likely fall short of meeting the approximate 50–70 grams of protein needed by active women and 70–90 grams of protein needed by men. See the worksheet "How to balance your protein intake" (page 59) to help you calculate your protein needs.

Note that a protein-deficient diet can also lack iron (prevents anemia) and zinc (helps with healing). I will discuss these minerals later.

The key to eating a high quality vegetarian diet is to eat a variety of foods that contain a variety of the eight essential amino acids needed for building protein. You can do that by simply eating a variety of grains, beans, legumes, nuts, seeds, soy and dairy products during meals and snacks over the course of the day.

Beans

For vegetarian marathoners, beans are not only a good source of protein, but also of carbohydrates, B-vitamins (such as folic acid), and fiber. When added to an overall lowfat diet, they may help lower elevated blood cholesterol levels.

The problem with beans is flatulence; some runners become gas propelled! If beans cause you intestinal problems, eat small amounts. If you cook your own beans, be sure to soak them long enough before cooking. You can also try Beano, a product that when added to beans helps reduce gas formation.

If you want to learn how to include more beans in your sports diet, here are a few suggestions:

- Sauté garlic and onions in a little oil; add canned, drained beans (whole or mashed); and heat together.
- Add beans to salads, spaghetti sauce, soups, and stews for a protein booster.
- In a blender, mix black beans, salsa, and cheese. Heat in the microwave and use as a dip or on top of tortillas or potatoes.

Red Meat: Eat or Avoid...?

Red meats such as beef and lamb are indisputably excellent sources of high-quality protein. They are also rich in iron and zinc, two minerals important for optimal health and athletic performance. Yet, some meat-eating marathoners are a bit unsure if eating red meat is a positive addition to their sports diet. If you wonder whether or not you should eat or avoid red meat, know that the answer is not a simple yes or no but rather a weighing of nutrition facts, ethical concerns, personal values, and dedication to making appropriate food choices. Yes, you can get the nutrients needed to support your sports program from non red-meat sources, but you have to make the effort to do so. The following facts can help you decide if tucking two to four small (3 to 4 ounce) portions of red meat per week into your meals might enhance the quality of your diet.

 It is easy to get enough carbs, but getting enough protein makes a big difference in my day-to-day performance.

Jonathan Dietrich,
Washington, DC

Meat and cholesterol: Meat, like chicken, fish, and other animal products, contains cholesterol because cholesterol is a part of animal cells; plant cells contain no cholesterol. Most animal proteins have similar cholesterol values: 70–80 milligrams of cholesterol per four ounce serving of red meat, poultry, and fish.

Given that the American Heart Association recommends that healthy people with normal blood cholesterol levels eat less than 300 milligrams of cholesterol per day, small portions of red meat can certainly fit those requirements. Marathoners who know their blood cholesterol number can make better personalized dietary decisions about how much dietary cholesterol is appropriate for their bodies.

Note that the cholesterol content of meat is of less concern than the fat content. Fatty meats such as greasy hamburgers, pepperoni, juicy steaks, and sausage are

Chicken Again?

Chicken has less saturated fat than many cuts of red meat, hence can be a good alternative for dinner. But if you are tired of eating yet another boring chicken breast, here are some simple ideas to spice it up:

• Spread with mustard and sprinkle with Parmesan cheese
• Spread with honey and sprinkle with curry powder
• Marinate for an hour or overnight in Italian dressing
• Spread with honey mustard

Place in baking pan (lined with foil for easy clean up) and bake uncovered at 350°F (175°C) for 20 to 30 minutes.

the real dietary no-nos. Lean meats—London broil, extra-lean hamburger, top round roast beef—can fit into a heart-healthy sports diet in appropriate amounts.

Meat and iron: Adequate iron in your sports diet is important to prevent anemia. Without question, the iron in red meat is more easily absorbed than that in popular vegetarian sources of iron (e.g., beans, raisins, spinach). In a study of eighteen women runners who consumed the recommended daily allowance for iron, eight of the nine women who ate no red meat (but did eat chicken and fish) had depleted iron stores as compared to only two of the nine red-meat eaters.

If you eat an iron-poor diet and are tempted to simply take an iron supplement, note that animal iron is absorbed better the iron in a pill. But any iron is better than no iron.

How to Boost Your Iron Intake

• The recommended intake for iron is 8 milligrams for men and 18 milligrams for women per day. Women have higher iron needs to replace the iron lost from menstrual bleeding. Women who are post-menopausal require only 8 milligrams of iron per day.
• Iron from animal products is absorbed better than that from plant products.
• A source of vitamin C at each meal enhances iron absorption.

Animal Sources (best absorbed)	Iron (mg)
Beef, 4 oz (120 g)	2
Pork, 4 oz (120 g)	1
Chicken breast, 4 oz (120 g)	1
Chicken leg, 4 oz (120 g)	1.5
Salmon, 4 oz (120 g)	1

Fruits

Prunes, 5	1
Raisins, 1/3 cup (45 g)	1

Vegetables

Spinach, 1/2 cup (100 g) cooked	3
Broccoli, 1 cup (180 g) cooked	1

Beans

Kidney, 1/2 cup (130 g)	2.5
Tofu, 1/2 cake (120 g)	2

Grains

Cereal, 100% iron fortified 1 oz (30 g)	18
Spaghetti, 1 cup cooked (140 g)	2
Bread, 1 oz (30 g) slice, enriched	1

Other

Molasses, blackstrap, 1 tablespoon (15 g)	3.5
Wheat germ, 1/4 cup (30 g)	2

Meat and zinc: Zinc is important for healing both the minor damage that occurs with daily training as well as major injuries and ailments. It is best found in iron-rich foods (e.g., red meat). Diets deficient in iron may then also be deficient in zinc. Like iron, the zinc in animal products is absorbed better than that in vegetable foods or supplements.

Meat and amenorrhea: Female runners who have amenorrhea and have stopped getting their menstrual period commonly eat no red meat. In one study, none of the amenorrheic runners ate red meat as compared to 44 percent of the runners with regular menses.

The question remains unanswered: Are these amenorrheic athletes simply protein deficient or is there a meat factor that affects the hormones involved with menstruation? Amenorrhea is a sign of poor health and loss of menses coincides with a higher rate of stress fractures. Hence, women who do not menstruate should carefully evaluate the adequacy of their diet. A sports dietitian can help them determine if their diet includes adequate protein, calories, and other nutrients. Refer to chapter 16 for more information.

How to Boost Your Zinc Intake

- The recommended intake for zinc is 8 milligrams for women and 11 milligrams for men per day.
- Animal foods, including seafood, are the best sources of zinc.

Animal Sources	Zinc (mg)
Beef, tenderloin, 4 ounces (120 g)	7
Chicken leg, 4 ounces (120 g)	3.5
Pork loin, 4 ounces (120 g)	3
Chicken breast, 4 ounces (120 g)	1
Cheese, 1 ounce (30 g)	1
Milk, 1 cup (240 ml)	1
Oysters, 6 medium (3 oz; 90 g)	75 (!)
Tuna, 1 can (6 oz; 170 g)	2
Clams, 9 small (3 oz; 90 g)	1

Plant Sources	
Wheat germ, 1/4 cup (30 g)	3.5
Lentils, 1 cup (200 g)	2.5
Almonds, 1 oz (30 g)	1
Garbanzo beans, 1/2 cup (100 g)	1
Spinach, 1 cup (200 g) cooked	0.7
Peanut butter, 1 tablespoon (15 g)	0.5
Bread, 1 slice (30 g), whole wheat	0.5

Hormones in meats: Fears abound regarding hormones given to cattle to enhance their growth. The U.S. Department of Agriculture claims the amount of hormones used is far less than one might get in the birth control pill, or even in a cup of coleslaw, for that matter. You can always buy meat at the natural food store to be on the safe side.

Fish: A super-protein

The protein in fish is among the most healthful animal sources of protein. That's because fish is low in saturated fat, the kind of fat that is associated with heart disease. And, fish rich in omega-3 fat, the good fat that makes human blood less likely to form clots that cause heart attacks and strokes. The American Heart

Why Chicken Has Light and Dark Meat

The white and dark meat in chicken (and turkey) is a handy example of the two kinds of muscle fibers that help you exercise:

- Fast-twitch fibers (white breast meat) are used for quick bursts of energy
- Slow-twitch fibers (dark leg, thigh, and wing meat) function best for endurance exercise.

Elite marathon runners tend to have the right combination of both—a high proportion of slow-twitch fibers for the long run, but also enough fast-twitch fibers for the sprint to the finish.

Slow-twitch muscles, more so than fast-twitch, rely on fat for fuel. This is why dark meat contains more fat than the white meat. On the plus side, dark meat also contains more nutrients—iron, zinc, and B-vitamins, many of the same nutrients found in red meats.

Chicken, without skin, 4 oz (120) cooked	Calories	Fat (g)	Iron (g)
Breast, white meat	180	4	1.2
Thigh, dark meat	235	12	1.5
Leg, dark meat	200	9	1.3

If you do not eat red meats, you might want to include more dark meat from chicken or turkey in your sports diet. For the small price of a few grams of fat, you'll get more nutritional value. If you want to cut back on fat, eliminate the skin—the fattiest part of poultry.

Association (AHA) recommends eating two fish meals per week, particularly oily fish, such as trout, wild or canned salmon, light tuna, sardines, and herring.

Eating fish comes with risks related to mercury and PCBs (polychlorinated biphenyls). The Food and Drug Administration (FDA) and the Environmental Protection Agency (EPA) advise women who may become pregnant or who currently are pregnant or breast feeding-and their young children-to avoid the fish highest in mercury (shark, swordfish, king mackerel (ono), tilefish). Large amounts of methylmercury can harm an unborn or young child's developing nervous system, resulting in problems with IQ, attention, reading, and memory. But everyone—including pregnant women—can safely enjoy up to twelve ounces (two or three fish meals) per week of low-mercury fish and shellfish: shrimp, salmon, pollock, catfish, and canned light tuna.

The health benefits of eating fish generally far outweigh the risks. But take note: if you are into sport-fishing, sushi-eating, having tuna for lunch every day, and enjoying high-mercury fish several times a week, the mercury can accumulate in your body and might create health problems. The trick to eating fish is to eat it in moderation and to consume a variety of different fish, with a focus on the smaller fish. Each week, enjoy a meal with oily fish (salmon, blue fish) and another with low-mercury fish (pollock, sole). Be moderate, and you'll get hooked with good health.

Strong muscles are important for marathon success. Be sure to get enough protein by eating protein-rich foods at two meals per day.

Protein Bars

When you are on the run and grabbing meals, a protein bar can be a convenient way to get hassle-free, lowfat protein. But because it is an engineered food, it lacks the wholesome goodness and yet-unidentified compounds that Nature puts in all natural sources of protein. Most protein bars include protein from whey or casein (milk is about 20% whey, 80% casein), soy and/or egg—all of which are excellent sources of amino acids. Some of the bars are handy snacks, others are hefty enough to be a meal replacement. They fall into the category of "convenient" but not "necessary."

Cooking Fish

Although cooking fish is simple, many marathoners eat fish only in restaurants because they don't know how to cook it. My advice: learn how to cook fish so you'll enjoy it more often as a great source of protein with a bonus of health-protective fish oils.

Here are some fish tips:
- Buy fresh fish that has no "fishy" odor. Ask to smell the fish before purchasing it. Fishy odor comes only with age and bacterial contamination. If you end up with fishy fish, rid your hands of any fishy smell by rubbing them with lemon juice or vinegar, and then washing them.
- Seasonings that go well with fish include lemon, dill, basil, rosemary, and parsley (and paprika for color).
- When grilling, sautéing or broiling fish, allow 10 minutes cooking time per inch of thickness. Fold thin parts under to make the fish as even a thickness as possible. As fish cooks, the flesh turns from translucent to opaque white, similar to egg whites.
- To test if done, gently pull the fish apart with a fork. It should flake easily and no longer be translucent. Do not overcook fish. Perfectly cooked fish is moist and has a delicate flavor, unlike overcooked fish that is dry and tasteless.
- If possible, cook fish in its serving dish (or in foil); fish is fragile and more attractive the less it is handled.

Summary

Lean meat is a convenient, nutrient-dense sports food. The fat in greasy meats, not the red meat itself, is the primary health culprit. Chicken and fish are lower fat alternatives, with fish being the the healthiest choice of all. If you prefer a vegetarian diet, just be sure to have a protein-rich food with each meal. "Vegetarians" who simply eliminate meat and make no effort to include alternate plant sources of protein, iron, and zinc can suffer from dietary deficiencies that hurt their sports performance. Protein bars can be a handy "emergency food" when you are eating on the run and your protein needs would otherwise be neglected.

Turkey Chili

A hearty bowl of chili is a welcome recovery food after chilly winter run. Chili provides a nice combination of carbs (from the beans and vegetables) to refuel muscles, and protein (from the turkey, and beans) to repair muscles. If you prefer to skip the turkey, simply add another can of beans.

This chili recipe is deliciously different. The secret ingredient is pineapple salsa (available from Trader Joe's). Any type of fruit salsa will yield an equally tasty meal.

If you cannot find roasted diced tomatoes, simply use whatever type of canned, diced or pureed tomato product is handy.

2 pounds (1 kg) ground turkey
2 tablespoons (30 ml) oil, preferably olive or canola
1 onion
3/4 pound (12 ounces; 340 g) baby carrots
1 red pepper
1 15.5 ounce (440 g) can red kidney beans
2 28-ounce (785 g) cans of roasted, diced tomatoes
2 12-ounce (335 g) jars of pineapple salsa
1/2 teaspoon (1 g) cinnamon
1 6-ounce (170 g) can tomato paste mixed with 8 ounces of water
Salt, as desired

1. Brown the turkey in one tablespoon of oil, drain, and set aside.
2. In a mini Cuisinart, chop up quartered onion, carrots and red pepper. (If you do not have a Cuisinart, chop them finely by hand.)
3. Sauté the vegetables together in another tablespoon of olive oil.
4. Add tomatoes, salsa, and seasoning. Bring to a boil and simmer. Make sure carrots are cooked through. Add turkey and tomato paste. Cook as long as desired.

Yield: 6 hearty servings
Total Calories: 2,700
Calories per serving: 450
42 g Carbohydrate
37 g Protein
15 g Fat

Recipe courtesy of Aly Wagner. Reprinted with permission from *Food Guide for Soccer: Tips and Recipes from the Pros* by Gloria Averbuch and Nancy Clark.

Fats and Your
Sports Diet

Eat fat, get fat. Eat fat, clog your arteries. Eat fat, have a heart attack. Eat fat, run slowly. I'm sure you've heard this anti-fat chatter. While there is an element of truth in some of these statements, there is also room for more education. Let's look at the whole picture.

While dietary fat used to be considered bad, we now know that all fats are not created equal. The hard, saturated fat in beef, butter, and cheese is the "bad" fat, as are the trans- (partially hydrogenated) fats in commercially baked goods. The soft, liquid polyunsaturated and monounsaturated fats in fish, olives, and nuts are the "good" fats, an essential nutrient needed for overall good health. Hence, there's no need to avoid all fat like the plague.

Olive oil, for example, is health-protective; it is the foundation of the acclaimed heart-healthy Mediterranean Diet. For centuries, native Italians and Greeks have enjoyed good health and a 40 percent fat diet. In general, I recommend that healthy marathoners target a sports diet with about 25 percent of the calories from (primarily healthful) fat. This:

- is in keeping with the American Heart Association's recommendation for a diet with 25 to 35 percent of the calories from fat.
- allows for adequate calories from carbohydrates (55–65 percent of total calories) and proteins (10–15 percent of total calories).
- enhances absorption of the fat-soluble vitamins, including vitamin E (an anti-oxidant thought to have a health-protective effect).
- allows for easier participation in life (i.e., eating at a party, enjoying a cookie guilt-free).

How does 25-percent fat translate into food? Let's say you have 1,800 calories a day in your calorie budget (this would be a reducing diet for most female marathoners):

25% x 1,800 total calories =
450 calories a day of fat.

There are 9 calories in one gram of fat, so—

450 calories divided by 9 calories/gram =
50 grams of fat in your daily fat budget.

A 25-percent-fat diet includes a reasonable amount of fat and lets you enjoy a little fat at each meal. Preferably, you'll choose fats that have positive health value such as olive oil, salmon and other oily fish, all-natural peanut butter, nuts, and tuna with light mayonnaise. But, if you do have the occasional hankering for a big burger with 25 grams of fat and 500 calories, simply fit it into your day's fat and calorie budget *and balance the rest of the day's meals.* (Refer to chapter 14 to determine your calorie needs.)

Fat Guidelines

The following guidelines can help you appropriately budget fat into your food plan.

Calories per day	Fat grams per day (for 25-percent-fat diet)
1,600	45
1,800	50
2,000	55
2,200	60
2,400	65

Fat Content of Some Common Foods

Food	Serving size	Fat (grams)	Calories
Dairy products			
Milk, whole (3.5% fat)	1 cup (240 ml)	8	150
reduced-fat (2% fat)	"	5	120
lowfat (1% fat)	"	2	100
fat-free (0% fat)	"	—	80
Cheese			
Cheddar	1 oz. (30 g)	9	110
reduced-fat	"	5	90
mozzarella, part-skim	"	5	80
cottage cheese (4% fat)	1/2 cup (120 g)	5	120
lowfat cottage cheese(2% fat)	"	2	90
Cream cheese, regular	1 oz. (2 tbsp.; 30 g)	10	100
Cream cheese, light	1 oz. (2 tbsp.; 30 g)	5	60
Ice cream, gourmet	1/2 cup (100 g)	15	250
Ice cream, standard	1/2 cup (80 g)	8	150
Ice cream, light	1/2 cup (70 g)	3	110
Frozen yogurt, lowfat	1/2 cup (70 g)	2	120
Frozen yogurt, fat-free	1/2 cup (90 g)	—	100
Animal proteins			
Beef, regular hamburger	4 oz. cooked (120 g)	24	330
Beef, flank steak	4 oz. cooked (120 g)	12	235
Beef, eye of round	4 oz. cooked (120 g)	6	200

Food	Serving size	Fat (grams)	Calories
Chicken, breast, no skin	4 oz. cooked (120 g)	5	200
Chicken, thigh, no skin	4 oz. cooked (120 g)	11	235
Fish, haddock	4 oz. cooked (120 g)	1	125
swordfish	4 oz. cooked (120 g)	6	175

Vegetable proteins

Food	Serving size	Fat (grams)	Calories
Beans, kidney	1/2 cup cooked (100 g)	—	110
Lentils	1/2 cup cooked	—	110
Tofu	4 oz. (120 g)	5	90
Peanut butter	1 tbsp. (15 g)	8	95

Fats

Food	Serving size	Fat (grams)	Calories
Butter	1 tbsp (15 g)	12	108
Margarine	1 tbsp (15 g)	11	102
Oil, olive	1 tbsp (15 g)	13	120
Mayonnaise	1 tbsp (15 g)	11	100

Grains

Food	Serving size	Fat (grams)	Calories
Bread, whole wheat	1 large slice (30 g)	1	90
Crackers, Saltines	5	2	60
Crackers, Ritz	5	4	80
Rice cakes	1	—	35
Cereal, shredded wheat	1 oz. (2/3 cup; 30 g)	—	90
Granola	1 oz. (1/4 cup; 30 g)	6	130
Oatmeal	1 oz. (1/3 cup; 30 g) dry	2	100
Spaghetti, plain	2 oz. dry (1 cup cooked; 140 g)	1	210
Rice	2 oz. dry (1 cup cooked; 160 g)	—	200

Fast foods

Food	Serving size	Fat (grams)	Calories
Big Mac	1	29	540
Egg McMuffin	1	12	300
French fries	small	11	230
KFC Fried chicken	breast	15	320
Pizza, cheese	1 slice large	10-13	250

Food	Serving size	Fat (grams)	Calories

Snacks, Treats

Food	Serving size	Fat (grams)	Calories
Cookie, Chips Ahoy	1 (1/2 oz.; 15 g)	3	55
Fig Newton	1 (1/2 oz.; 15 g)	1	55
Brownie, from mix	1 small	5	140
Graham crackers	2 squares	1	60
Potato chips	1 oz. (about 18 chips)	9	150
Pretzels	1 oz. (30 g)	1	110
Milky Way	1.75 oz. bar (50 g)	8	220
M&Ms w/ peanuts	1.75 oz. (50 g) bag	13	250
Reese's Peanut Butter Cups	1.6 oz. (2 cups; 45 g)	15	280

Fruits and Vegetables

Most varieties   negligible fat

Fear of Fat

Without question, fat imparts a tempting taste, texture, and aroma and helps make food taste great. That's why fatty foods can be hard to resist and easily enjoyed to excess. Although excess fat-calories can easily turn into body fat, note the "eat fat, get fat" theory is false. Many active people eat appropriate amounts of fat and stay thin. They simply don't overeat calories.

If you are weight-conscious and obsess about every gram of fat to the extent you have a fat phobia, your fear of fat may be exaggerated! A little fat can actually aid in weight reduction because it takes longer to empty from the stomach—and offers that nice feeling of being satisfied after a meal. For example, you may have less desire to keep munching on, let's say, yet-another rice cake if you start off eating a rice cake with a little peanut butter.

Believe it or not, many of my clients have lost body fat after they reintroduced an appropriate amount of dietary fat back into their fat-free regimen. Refer to the weight reduction information in chapter 15 for additional help with resolving your "eat fat, get fat" fears.

As a marathoner, you want to include a little fat in each meal to not only help absorb certain vitamins but also to enhance performance. Runners who boosted their intake of healthful fat from 17% of calories to 30% of calories were not only able to run longer but also had less inflammation afterwards. Fat is certainly NOT a four-letter word!

Summary

Marathoners who include some fat in their daily training diet perform better than those who try to exclude fat. Obviously, choosing more of the healthful fats— olive oil, canola oil, nuts, peanut butter, salmon—is preferable to loading up on the saturated fat in buttery cookies, greasy burgers, and gourmet ice cream. But all fats eaten in moderation can be balanced into an overall healthful and carbohydrate-rich sports diet.

OVEN-FRIED CHICKEN

Deep fat fried chicken is popular with many marathoners, but it fails to be the healthiest of sports foods. This recipe offers a lower-fat alternative that will get "thumbs up" from even fussy eaters. The recipe is reprinted with permission from the May/June 1999 issue of *Cook's Illustrated*, a cooking magazine that I highly recommend if you want to learn more about the what's, how's, and why's of cooking (www.cooksillustrated.com).

1 box (5 ounces) Melba toast
2 to 4 tablespoons olive or canola oil
2 egg whites or 1 egg
4 boneless, skinless chicken breasts
Optional: 1 tablespoon Dijon mustard, salt, pepper

1. Heat oven to 400°F (200°C). Set a wire rack in a shallow baking pan. If desired, line the pan with foil for ease with clean-up. Cooking the chicken on a rack allows air to circulate on all sides, resulting in a crisper chicken without turning.
2. Put the Melba toast into a heavy-duty plastic bag, seal, and pound with a rolling pin or other hard object (wine bottle, can, fist). Leave some crumbs the size of small pebbles to add crunchiness.
3. Put the crumbs in a shallow dish and drizzle the oil over them, tossing well to distribute the oil evenly.
4. Beat the egg in a medium bowl. Add optional seasonings as desired.
5. One piece of chicken at a time, coat the chicken with the egg mixture, then place in the crumbs. Sprinkle the crumbs over the flesh and press them in.
6. Gently shake off excess crumbs and place the chicken on the rack.
7. Bake about 40 minutes, or until the coating is a deep brown and the juices run clear when the meat is slit with a knife.

Yield: 4 servings
Total calories: 1,200
Calories per serving: 300

Carbohydrate 12 g
Protein 40 g
Fat 10 g

Reprinted, by permission, from *Cook's Illustrated,* May/June 1999.
www.cooksillustrated.com

Chapter 8

Water and
Sports Drinks

Today's marathoners know that preventing dehydration is an important part of their training and racing program. But that wasn't always the case. For example, in 1953, running regulations stated that marathoners could take water only after 9.3 miles. This contrasts to 2010, when most marathons provide water stations every one or two miles along their courses.

While dehydration is the main concern for marathoners, drinking too much water has created medical problems in a few overzealous drinkers. So what's the right balance of water and exercise? The Association of International Marathon Directors recommends you drink according to thirst. Thirst is a clear signal your body needs fluids. If you have trouble honoring thirst, then follow The American College of Sports Medicine's recommendation to learn your personal sweat rate.

To determine how much you should drink during exercise, weigh yourself (without clothes) before and after an hour of training. If you have lost one pound (16 ounces; 450 mg) in one hour, you've lost one pint (16 ounces; 450 ml) of sweat, and should plan to drink accordingly during the next exercise session—at least 8 ounces (225 ml) every half-hour. You may need to weigh yourself at different seasons, because your sweat losses in winter might be less than in summer. But if you are overdressed for a winter training run, or are sweating hard during a treadmill run at the gym, your sweat losses might be even higher!

Strive to lose no more than 2 percent of your body weight per exercise session. That is, if you weigh 150 pounds (68 kg), try not to lose more than 3 pounds (1.5 kg) of sweat during a workout. Practice drinking fluids during training runs, so on marathon day you'll be familiar with the skills involved in drinking during exercise as well as your body's capacity for fluids. Go to the marathon's website, so you can find out which sports drink will be offered. Practice drinking that brand during long training runs, so you can learn 1) if it settles well and 2) how much of it you can tolerate.

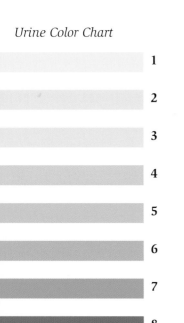

Urine Color Chart

1
2
3
4
5
6
7
8

Dehydration slows you down, and in extreme cases, can contribute to medical problems. If you replace fluid losses poorly during training and are chronically dehydrated, you'll tend to experience needless fatigue and lethargy. Don't let that happen! You can tell if you are well hydrated on a daily basis by monitoring your urine:
- You should urinate frequently (every 2 to 4 hours) throughout the day.
- The urine should be clear and of significant volume.
- Your morning urine should not be dark and concentrated. Use the Urine Color Char to help determine if you have been consuming enough fluids to stay well hydrated. If your urine is darker than 3, drink more!

Reprint permission granted by L. Armstrong PhD

Sports Drinks

Although water is an adequate fluid replacer during short runs and walks (less than an hour), sports drinks are helpful during training sessions that last longer than 60 to 90 minutes. You'll perform better and feel better if you drink more than just plain water. Sports drinks provide:

- small amounts of *carbohydrates* to fuel your mind and muscles
- *sodium* to enhance water absorption and retention
- *water* to replace sweat losses

In the summer, before my long runs, I drive along the course and hide water bottles in the shrubs and behind telephone poles. Most of the time, the water is there when I run by and need a drink.

Amy Singer, Seattle, WA

With the multitude of sports drinks on the market, it is easy to feel confused about what's best to drink, and to wonder which ones are better than the others. The bottom line is that you should choose the drink that you prefer; there are no significant advantages to one over the other. With luck, the one you prefer is the one that will be available during your marathon!

People's stomach function during exercise varies enormously. That's why some people prefer plain water, others seek out a particular brand of sports drink, and some make their own concoction. The most important point is to *drink enough.* Any fluid, be it water or sports drink, is better than no fluid during extended exercise.

If you prefer to abstain from sports drinks, the alternate way to consume adequate water and carbs is to have one or two glasses of water pre-run along with a snack and then drink water and enjoy jellybeans, gels, energy bars and other sources of carbs during the long run. See chapter 10 for more information about Foods and Fluids during Long Walks and Runs.

I've solved the problem of getting sticky from sports drinks that splash all over me when I'm running in a race: I cut a straw in half and tuck it under my watchband. I then use the straw to drink from the cup while I'm running. I'm sure I end up drinking more fluids. The trick is to not drop the straw!

Bill Franks,
Sanbornton, NH

Sodium Replacement

When you sweat, you lose sodium, an electrolyte (electrically charged particle) that helps maintain proper water balance in your tissues. Most runners don't have to worry about replacing sodium during exercise because the losses are generally too small to cause a deficit that will hurt performance and/or health. But, if you will be exercising for more than four hours, sodium loss can become problematic. Your best bet during extended exercise is to choose sports drinks and foods that contain sodium. The standard sports drink alone does not protect

Comparing Fluid Replacements

Beverage (8 oz)	Calories	Sodium (mg)	Potassium (mg)
Gatorade G2	20	110	30
Gatorade	50	110	30
Gatorade Endurance	50	200	90
PowerAde	70	55	30
Cola	100	5	—
Beer	100	12	60
Orange juice	110	2	475
Cranapple juice	175	5	70
Chicken Broth	15	930	70
Possible losses in 2 hours	1,000	1,000	300

against hyponatremia because a sports drink offers far more water than sodium. The typical sports drink may have only 1/5th the concentration of normal blood serum. The sodium is added primarily to enhance retention of the water in your body, not to replace the sodium lost in sweat.

Marathoners who drink excessive water and/or sports drinks dilute the sodium outside the cells; this causes too much water to seep into cells and the cells swell—including the cells in the brain. Symptoms that progressively appear include feeling weak, groggy, nauseous, incoherent, and ultimately stumbling, seizures, coma, and death. This is preventable!

Salt: Shake It or Leave It?

The rule of thumb is to add extra salt to your diet if you have lost more than four to six pounds of sweat (3 to 4 percent of your body weight pre- to post-exercise). Salty sweaters (who end up with a crust of salt on their skin after a hard workout) and heavy sweaters (who lose more than two pounds of sweat per hour) should pay close attention to their sodium intake—particularly if they are not acclimatized to running in the heat. For example, if you are training in the winter for a marathon that happens to land on an exceptionally warm spring day, you might need extra sodium during the marathon. Some marathoners choose Gatorade's Endurance Formula, while others eat pretzels, drink V-8 juice along the way, or lick salt from little packets (from a restaurant).

In general, most marathoners consume adequate sodium on a daily basis, even without adding salt to their food. For example, you get sodium via bread

(150 mg/slice), cheese (220 mg/oz (30 g)), eggs (60 mg/egg), and yogurt (125 mg/8 oz/240 ml). Athletes who are extreme sweaters may need more sodium, but generally consume more, particularly if they eat fast foods. Just two slices of cheese pizza (1,200 mg) or a Whopper (970 mg) can easily replace sodium losses; no sweat!

If you crave salt, you should eat it. Salt cravings signal that your body wants salt. If you hanker for some pretzels or salty foods after a long run, eat them. Soup can be a welcoming recovery food after a cold-weather run; the broth provides warmth, water, and salt.

How to Keep Your Cool

The following true-false quiz is designed to test your knowledge about fluid replacement and help you survive the heat in good health and with high energy.

Drinking a slushie before hot-weather running will help keep you cool.
True. If you have to run in the heat, pre-cooling your body with a big slushie can help you stay cooler for a little longer. You might also want to pre-freeze a water bottle that you can carry with you in a fuel belt, so you can enjoy cold water during the run.

Soda is a poor choice during exercise because the carbon dioxide in the bubbles will slow you down.
False. Historically, athletes were always warned to "de-fizz" carbonated beverages taken during exercise, fearing that the carbonation would interfere with oxygen transport and would also hurt performance. Not the case. Studies comparing carbonated and non-carbonated soft drinks suggest bubbles will not hurt your performance nor result in stomach discomfort.

Don't bother to drink during a run that is shorter than an hour because the fluid has too little time to get into your system.
False. According to Larry Armstrong, exercise physiologist at the University of Connecticut, water can travel from stomach to skin in only 9 to 18 minutes after drinking. This water is essential for dissipating the 15 to 20 times more heat you produce during exercise as compared to that produced while you are at rest.

Beer is an appropriate recovery fluid.
False. Although beer is a popular post-exercise recovery drink, its alcohol content has both a dehydrating and depressant effect. If you drink beer on an empty stomach (as commonly happens post-run), you can quickly negate the pleasurable "natural high" that you would otherwise enjoy. Wise beer-drinkers first have 1 to 2 glasses of water and eat some carbohydrate-rich foods (e.g., pretzels, pizza, crackers) and then they enjoy a beer or two in moderation.

Homemade Sports Drink

The main ingredients in commercial fluid replacers are:

Sugar. Sports drinks are 5 to 7 percent sugar; they contain about 12 grams of carbohydrate (50 calories) per 8 ounces—this is equal to 3 teaspoons (8 g) of sugar per cup.

Sodium. They contain 50 to 110 milligrams of sodium per 8 ounces—this is equal to 1/8 teaspoon or 1 pinch of salt per cup.
This recipe comes close enough. Give it a try if you want a low-cost fluid replacer.

1/4 cup (30 g) sugar
1/4 teaspoon (1 g) salt
1/4 cup (60 ml) orange juice
3 1/2 cups (840 ml) cold water

1. In the bottom of a one-quart (one-liter) bottle, dissolve the sugar in a little bit of hot water.
2. Add the salt and juice.
3. Add the cold water.
4. Quench that thirst!

YIELD: 1 quart or 4 8-oz. servings (~ 1 liter; 4 240-ml)
Total calories: 200
Calories per serving: 50

Carb 12 g
Pro 0 g
Fat 0 g
Sodium 110 mg
Potassium 30 mg

Section III
Fueling Long Walks and Runs

Chapter 9

Fueling Before You Exercise

One of the biggest mistakes made by novice marathoners (in particular, weight-conscious marathoners) is to train on empty. They think this will help them lose fat and run faster. Wrong! Just as your car works best with gas in its tank, your body works best when it has been appropriately fueled.

But food can sometimes be a problem for people who fear food-related upset stomachs that interfere with exercise. Running and fast walking jostles your stomach and enhances your risk of intestinal distress. An estimated 25 to 30 percent of runners may experience abdominal cramps, diarrhea, and/or the need for pit stops during or immediately after running.

Pre-exercise food can offer you a competitive edge that contributes to greater stamina and endurance. If you have always abstained from eating a little bit of something before you exercise, I encourage you to try a light snack. You might be pleasantly surprised by the benefits that come from fueling up rather than running on empty.

Because eating ability and food preferences vary in relation to the type and intensity of exercise and the time of day, all marathoners should practice pre-exercise eating and remember that you are training your intestinal tract as well as your heart, lungs, and muscles. During training, you will learn through trial and error:

- what foods work best for your body
- when you should eat them
- what amounts are appropriate

Any of the following recommendations regarding pre-exercise eating should be pondered and experimented with during long runs, *not on marathon day*. You are an experiment of one; that is, only you can best determine what works best for your body. And remember, food that you can tolerate on a normal training run may become intolerable during a marathon. Chalk that up to pre-event nervousness, not the food itself.

I emphasize *experiment during training* because here's what typically happens:

Marathoners read advertisements about special sports drinks, energy bars, supplements, or liquid meals. They are curious about trying these special products but because of their high price tag, they don't quite get around to buying them. Instead, they end up trying the free products provided by the sponsors on marathon day. In some instances they discover (much to their dismay) that for them the unfamiliar food causes an upset stomach, heartburn, diarrhea, or cramps. If they had sampled these new products during training, they would have known whether or not to use the race-day samples.

What (and whether) you eat before exercise will vary according to:

- *The type of exercise.* Pre-run food may make you uncomfortable, but pre-walk or pre-bike food might not cause any problems.
- *How hard you will be working.* You may be able to eat within ten minutes of an easy training run or an hour before a marathon, but need to plan for three hours before a track workout.
- *How nervous you are.* Nothing will settle well if your stomach is in knots.

The general rule of thumb is that the harder you exercise, the less likely you are to want to eat, and the more likely you need to allow ample time for food to digest between eating and exercising. Fast runners may feel nauseated at even the thought of pre-exercise food, but slow walkers will appreciate the added energy.

If you exercise at a pace that you can comfortably sustain for more than 30 minutes, you can digest food at the same time. At a training pace, the blood flow to your stomach is 60 to 70 percent of normal—adequate to maintain normal digestion processes.

If you are doing intense sprint work, your stomach essentially shuts down and gets only about 20 percent of its normal blood flow. This slows the digestion process so that pre-exercise food will jostle along for the ride and possibly "talk back." It may feel uncomfortable and cause indigestion or heartburn.

Five Benefits of Pre-exercise Fueling

If you are in the experimental stage of developing your pre-exercise food plan for various intensity walks or runs, as well as for a marathon, the following information provides some helpful facts about the benefits of pre-exercise food. This information can help you on marathon day when the right combination of food and fluids will make or break your ability to complete the distance comfortably.

1. *Pre-exercise food helps prevent low blood sugar.* Why suffer with light-headedness, needless fatigue,

I've trained my body to thrive on pre-exercise food. From the beginning of my running career, I have always run with food in my stomach. I'd eat meals and snacks with my children so that I could enjoy family time with them, and then I'd run at night. I now have an iron stomach. I can eat and run—nothing bothers me.

Hal Gabriel,
Newton, MA

One year, the guy who was driving me to the marathon stopped for donuts, so I got some too. That was a mistake because I generally have only toast. The donuts landed like lead sinkers. I was in good shape for the marathon, but too many donuts did me in.

Gerry Beagan,
North Kingston, RI

irritability, and inability to concentrate when you can prevent these symptoms of hypoglycemia?

The carbohydrates in your pre-exercise snack are important because they fuel not only your muscles but also your mind. Adequate carbohydrates help you think clearly because your brain fuels itself with glucose, the sugar in your blood that is derived from carbohydrates. As marathon legend Grete Waitz once commented, "Novice runners often fail to recognize how much mental energy and concentration is needed to run—especially to run a marathon."

Your blood glucose is maintained at a normal level by the release of glucose that is stored in your liver as glycogen. If you have low blood sugar or a low liver glycogen (as can happen before breakfast or in the afternoon if you fail to eat enough earlier in the day), your brain will be left unfed. You will feel tired and have trouble concentrating on the task at hand. You may feel like you've "hit the wall." Why suffer with needless fatigue when you can prevent (or at least, delay) fatigue by fueling yourself appropriately before you run?

If you run in the morning without consuming any fuel between your 7:00 p.m. dinner and your 7:00 a.m. run, you will likely to have to drag yourself through your workout. Similarly, if you choose to eat nothing between the pre-marathon pasta party and the late-morning start of the New York City Marathon or the Boston Marathon, you'll begin the event depleted and may end up devastated. Your blood sugar levels will have dropped, particularly if you tossed and turned all night with pre-race anxiety.

Some morning runners exercise with an empty stomach and report that they have plenty of energy. They have likely eaten a substantial dinner and/or done serious late-night snacking that bolstered their liver glycogen stores and reduced their need for a morning energizer. This is not bad or wrong, as long as this pattern works well for them. But, in general, runners who do most of their eating at the end of the day tend to have more body fat than those who fuel well during the day. (See Chapter 15. Weight and Marathoners for more information on weight management.)

2. *Pre-exercise food helps settle the stomach, absorbs some of the gastric juices, and abates hunger feelings.* For many people, the stress associated with competition stimulates gastric secretions and contributes to an "acid stomach." Eating a small amount of food can help alleviate that problem.

The caloric density of a snack or meal affects the rate at which the food leaves your stomach. This explains why you can exercise comfortably soon after snacking on a few crackers or a piece of fruit but are better off waiting three or four hours after a heartier meal.

The general pre-exercise "rule of thumb" is to allow:
• 3–4 hours for a large meal to digest
• 2–3 hours for a smaller meal

- 1–2 hours for a blended or liquid meal
- less than an hour for a small snack, as tolerated

Rather than eating a full breakfast before an 8:00 a.m. marathon, you might want to eat part of that breakfast the night before, prior to going to bed. (Experiment with this prior to long training runs.) This allows allow ample time for that food to digest and helps maintain a normal blood glucose level. You can then eat the second half of the breakfast at 6:00 a.m.

3. *Pre-exercise food fuels the muscles.* The food you eat even an hour before you exercise is digested into glucose and burned for energy. For example, one study showed that runners who ate 400 calories of sugar three hours before an easy four-hour run burned about 70 percent of the sugar. Without question, pre-run food that is well tolerated provides an energy boost that enhances stamina.

If you have trouble with solid foods such as a bagel, you might want to experiment with liquids, such as a fruit smoothie or a canned liquid meal such as Boost. One research study showed that a 450-calorie meal of steak, peas, and buttered bread took six hours to leave the stomach, whereas a blenderized variation of the same meal emptied from the stomach in four hours.

In general, carbohydrates are digested more easily than fatty foods. Lowfat foods and meals (such as those listed in the sidebar, High Carbohydrate Meal Suggestions, page 81) tend to digest easily and settle well. In comparison, high-fat-bacon-and-fried-egg breakfasts, greasy hamburgers, tuna subs loaded with mayonnaise, and grilled cheese sandwiches have been known to settle heavily and feel uncomfortable. Too much fat slows digestion, so the meal lingers longer in the stomach and may contribute to a weighed-down feeling.

A little fat, however, such as in a slice of lowfat cheese on toast, a skimming of peanut butter on a bagel, or the fat in some brands of energy bars, can be appropriate. It provides both sustained energy and satiety during long runs. Some marathoners break all the sports nutrition rules and still perform well with even very high-fat and protein-rich foods. After all, steak and eggs was the pre-marathon breakfast of champions for many years! Protein and fat offer sustained energy—the fuel you'll use three hours into the event!

4. *Pre-exercise beverages can provide fluids to fully hydrate your body as well as additional carbohydrates.* By tanking up on diluted juice or sports drinks before you exercise, you can help prevent dehydration as well as boost your carbohydrate and energy intake. Whereas you are unlikely to starve during the marathon, you may become seriously injured due to dehydration. The best pre-exercise fluid choices include water, sports drinks, diluted juices and even coffee or tea if you want a caffeine-boost.

> **All the experimenting for marathon day should have been completed at least four weeks prior to the marathon. During these final four weeks, you should fine tune what you've learned to be sure that your body can handle your choice of foods and fluids.**
>
> John Correia,
> San Diego, CA

Pre-exercise Meals

To be sufficiently fueled for long training runs and walks, hard track workouts, shorter races, or the marathon, eat according to this schedule. Always drink additional fluids with and between meals to ensure complete hydration. If you are overly nervous, stressed, or have a sensitive stomach prior to the event, you may have to abstain from food on the day of competition. If that's the case, be sure to eat extra food the day before.

Morning events:

The day before:	Minimal exercise
	Eat a hearty, carbohydrate-based lunch, dinner, and bedtime snack.
Race morning:	Eat a light snack/breakfast to abate hunger feelings and replenish liver glycogen stores.

Example:

Lunch:	Turkey sub, pretzels, cranberry juice
Dinner:	Spaghetti, with tomato sauce, a few meatballs, green beans, bread, frozen yogurt
Bedtime:	Bagel with (a little) peanut butter and jam, orange juice
Breakfast:	Oatmeal, banana

Afternoon events:

Day before:	Minimal exercise
	Eat a hearty carbohydrate-based dinner.
Race day:	Eat a hearty carbohydrate-based breakfast and a light lunch.

Example:

Dinner:	Fish, lots of rice, winter squash, rolls, fig bars, juice
Breakfast:	Pancakes, syrup, melon, lowfat milk
Lunch:	Chicken sandwich and/or minestrone soup, crackers

Evening events:

Day before:	Minimal exercise
	Eat carbohydrate-based meals.
Race day:	Eat a hearty carbohydrate-based breakfast and lunch, followed by a light snack 1 to 3 hours prior to the event.

Example:

Breakfast:	Grape-Nuts, (canned) peaches, lowfat milk, English Muffin, honey, orange juice
Lunch:	Big bagel with peanut butter, jelly, animal crackers, cranapple juice
Snack:	Energy bar, yogurt, banana as desired

High-Carbohydrate Meal Suggestions

Some high-carbohydrate meal suggestions the day before long training runs as well as the marathon itself include tried-and-true foods such as:

Breakfast: cold cereals, oatmeal and other hot cereals, bagels, English muffins, pancakes, French toast with syrup, jam, honey, fruit, juice

Lunch: sandwiches (with the bread being the "meat" of the sandwich), fruit, (not greasy) thick-crust pizza, hummus with pita, hearty bean- or broth-based soups with noodles, rice, vegetables

Dinner: Pasta-, potato- or rice-based entrées; veggies, breads, juice, fruit

Snacks: flavored yogurt, pretzels, crackers, fig bars, frozen yogurt, dry cereal, leftover pasta, zwieback, energy bars, simple biscuit-type cookies, animal crackers, canned and fresh fruits, juice

You should drink plenty of fluids not only before marathons and other races but also every day during training, in both hot weather and cold weather. You can confirm that you've had enough to drink by frequent urination and clear-colored urine. If your urine is dark and concentrated, you need more fluids. Refer to chapter 8 for more information on hydration.

5. *Pre-exercise food can pacify your mind with the knowledge that your body is well fueled.* Before a long training run or walk, and particularly before a marathon, you don't want to waste any energy wondering if you've eaten enough. Appropriate eating can resolve that concern!

Pre-exercise food has great psychological value. If you firmly believe that a specific food or meal will enhance your performance, then it probably will. Your mind has a powerful effect on your body's ability to perform at its best. If you do have a "magic food" that assures athletic excellence, you should take special care to be sure this food or meal is available prior to the race.

Summary

Whether you are a walker or a runner, pre-exercise food will help you better enjoy your marathon-training program. Just as you put gas in your car before you take it for a drive, you should put 100 to 300 calories of carbohydrate-rich food in your body before you exercise. You need to train your intestinal tract to tolerate this fuel, just as you are training your heart, lungs, and muscles to go the distance. Granted, each marathoner is an experiment of one, and some marathoners can tolerate food better than others; that's why you need to experiment during training to determine what pre-exercise menu works best for you.

Sugar and Spice Trail Mix

This crunchy munchie is a welcome snack for hungry marathoners who want something that's sweet, but not too sweet. Store the trail mix in individual portions in Ziploc bags, and keep it handy for a mid-afternoon energizer before you exercise, or for a travel-snack when you are on the road.

The recipe is from the American Heart Association's website: www.deliciousdecisions.org—a good source of many healthful yet tasty recipes.

3 cups (170 g) Oat Squares cereal
3 cups (170 g) mini-pretzels, salted or salt-free, as desired
2 tablespoons (30 g) tub margarine, melted
1 tablespoon (10 g) packed brown sugar
1/2 teaspoon (2.5 g) cinnamon
1 cup (140 g) dried fruit bits or raisins

1. Preheat oven to 325°F (160°C).
2. In a large plastic Zip-lock bag or plastic container with a cover, combine the oat squares and pretzels.
3. In a small bowl, stir together the melted margarine, brown sugar and cinnamon. Pour over the cereal mixture.
4. Seal the bag or container and shake gently until the mixture is well coated. Transfer to a baking sheet.
5. Bake, uncovered for 15 to 20 minutes, stirring once or twice.
6. Let cool, and then add the dried fruit.
7. Store in an airtight container or smaller single-serving baggies.

Yield: 10 servings (about 2/3 cup)
Total calories: 2,000
Calories per serving: 200

Carbohydrate: 40
Protein: 5
Fat: 2

Reprinted with permission from the American Heart Association and *Nancy Clark's Sports Nutrition Guidebook, Fourth Edition,* Human Kinetics, 2008.

RECIPE

Foods and Fluids During Long Walks and Runs

Whether you are hoping to complete the marathon in three hours or six hours, the single most important nutrition tip is to learn *during* training sessions how to eat for the marathon. Learn to eat early and often, and learn what types of foods and fluids your body can tolerate. As I've mentioned before, your training runs and walks are to train not only your heart, lungs, and muscles, but also your intestinal tract so you can keep yourself well fueled and hydrated. This will delay fatigue, prevent dehydration, and lower the risk of discomfort and undesired pit stops.

As an endurance athlete, your goals are to:
1) drink enough fluid to prevent dehydration (and not become overhydrated)
2) consume enough carbs to prevent hypoglycemia (low blood sugar).
You can succeed at meeting these goals by drinking carbohydrate-containing fluids (such as a sports drink) or by combining water with solid foods (water + energy bar). Although you'll rarely see elite runners consuming more than a sports drink, slower marathoners can do well with a variety of fluids and foods that they have used during training.

Beginning walkers, in particular, could carry with them a veritable picnic basket—energy bars, trail mix, sports drinks, even sandwiches and fruit—for any distance over 90 minutes. I've seen too many walkers dragging themselves along the course, drained of energy and dehydrated. Many are walking for over 8 hours, and they would have normally eaten at least two meals during that time frame.

Creating a Fueling Plan

During training and marathons, be sure to drink every 15 to 20 minutes. Remember, you want to *prevent* dehydration. Don't let yourself get too thirsty. By drinking on a schedule—let's say, a target of about 4 to 8 ounces (120-240 ml), that's 4 to 8 gulps, of water or sports drink every 15 to 20 minutes—you can minimize dehydration, maximize your performance, and reduce your recovery time.

As I talked about in chapter 8, learning your sweat rate helps you determine how much to drink—particularly if you sweat heavily. Be certain you make the effort to weigh yourself before and after a one-hour race-pace run or walk so you'll know how much sweat you lose (and need to replace): one pound of sweat = one pound of water lost (16 ounces; 480 g).

Start drinking within a half-hour to prevent dehydration; once you are dehydrated, you won't catch up. Losing only two percent of your body weight (3 pounds for a 150-pound person; 1.4 kg. for a 70 kg person) from sweating hurts your performance and upsets your ability to regulate your body temperature. (Refer to chapter 8 for more details.) To keep hydrated:
- If you are training with a group, take advantage of the water stations your coach has set up along the route.
- If you are in a race, find out in advance the location of each water station. If there is a water station every mile, you might want to drink at every other

station (every 15 to 20 minutes) or according to thirst.

- If you are training by yourself, set up your own water stops. This means planning a route that includes adequate water fountains, or driving the route before your run/walk and placing bottles filled with water or sports drinks in strategic locations.
- Take fluids with you. Some marathoners prefer to run with a Camelbak (water bladder that's worn like a backpack) or other portable hydration system.

Yes, you want to drink according to a schedule, but also pay attention to thirst. Don't force fluids. Drinking too much fluid to the point you feel the excess water sloshing around in your stomach also causes problems—nausea, if not hyponatremia (low blood sodium). The immediate solution is to stop drinking for a while. The long-term solution is to practice drinking during training, so your body can adapt to the appropriate fluid intake.

You will feel happier and more energetic if you can replace not only water but also carbohydrates while running or walking. These carbohydrates help to maintain a normal blood sugar level as well as provide a source of energy for muscles. Then, during the marathon, when you come to the 18- or 20-mile mark, you can breeze right though it to the finish—and avoid hitting "the wall."

Research suggests you might be able to increase your stamina by as much as 18 percent if you take in 0.5 grams of carbohydrate per pound of body weight (or 1 gram per kilogram) per hour of endurance exercise. For example, if you weigh 150 pounds, you should target about 75 grams of carbohydrates (300 calories) per hour. This could be:
- six 8-ounce glasses of a sports drink (50 calories per 8 ounces)

Popular Snacks During a Long Run

A plethora of commercial sports snacks are available for marathoners, yet "real foods" can work just as well. Experiment with a variety of textures (soft, hard, dry, moist) and flavors (sweet, sour, salty), knowing that tastes change over the course of 26.2 miles.

Solids:	Liquids:
Dried figs	Diluted, defizzed cola
Energy bar	Sports drinks
Bagel	Iced tea with honey
Tootsie Rolls	Diluted juice
Hard candies	Iced coffee with sugar
Mini chocolate bars	Applesauce (in a squeeze-pack)
Gummy candies	Honey sticks
Sports beans	Gels
Vanilla cookies	Water (with solid food)
Pretzels	Broth (for salt)

"During a marathon, I prefer Swedish fish (gummy candy) over the gels because, as some runners know, gels sometimes send runners to the porta-potties during the race. Swedish fish give me an immediate sugar-fix, take the edge off the light-headed feeling, and don't leave me feeling sick afterwards. You can even bite down on this candy and it will stay in your teeth to keep the glucose coming. Perhaps this is not so great for your teeth, but it works for me.

Valerie Watson, OH

Commercial Sports Foods

Ever feel confused by the plethora of commercial sports foods from which to choose? A multitude of businesses have jumped on the bandwagon to create products that appeal to a variety of athletes, from those with special dietary requests (such as gluten-free or vegan) to those who are just plain hungry and want a "politically correct" candy bar (Marathon Bar). When it comes to what to buy, there is no "best choice;" you simply need to experiment to determine what products satisfy your taste buds and settle well in your stomach. Most of the sports products claim to be easy to digest, but you will have to determine that for yourself!

Today's $2-billion-and-growing sports fuel industry is indeed booming. Busy athletes enjoy the convenience, taste and ease of using designer sports foods. While these commercial sports foods tend to be more about convenience than necessity, they can make fueling easier for busy marathoners. Just keep in mind "real food" (dried figs, gummy bears, chocolate milk) can do the same job at a lower price. After all, athletes managed to survive and perform well for years prior to the 1970's (when Gatorade became popular), 1980's (when PowerBar was introduced), and 1990's (when gels entered the sports scene). Certainly, there is a time and place for all of these products. Just be sure you maintain a foundation of wholesome foods in the midst of the engineered choices. There should be a few apple cores and banana peels along with the empty wrappers.

Below is an extensive (but incomplete) list of various types of assorted sports fuels and foods. Perhaps it will help you untangle the jungle of choices. Don't be swayed by a product's name; it might be more powerful than the sports food itself!

SPORTS DRINKS
With sodium (and perhaps other electrolytes):
Gatorade, PowerAde, Edge Energy, Hydro-Boom!, GU2O, CytoMax

All natural without dye/food coloring:
Carb BOOM! Electrolyte Sports Drink, First Endurance EFS, Clif Quench, Hammer Nutrition HEED, Recharge, Coconut Water

Extra sodium (Good idea if you plan to exercise for > 2 hours in the heat):
Gatorade Endurance, PowerBar Endurance, E-Fuel, First Endurance EFS, Clif Shot Electrolyte Drink, E-Load, Hydro Pro Cooler, Motor Tabs, GU Brew Electrolyte

Added "buffers:" Cytomax, Perpetuem, Revenge Sport

Extra carbs: Perpetuem, Carbo-Pro

Added protein (May reduce post-exercise muscle soreness);
Amino Vital, Perpetuem, Accelerade, Revenge Pro

Sports drinks for dieters (i.e., lower calorie):
G2, PowerAde Zero, Ultima Replenisher, Xtra LowOz, Propel, Nuun

GELS
(Test with these during training. They can taste very sweet and are common contributors to diarrhea)
Gu, Carb-BOOM!, Clif Shot, Honey Stinger (all natural)

Extra sodium: PowerBar Gel, Crank Sports e-Gel, EFS Liquid Shot, Gu Roctane

Added protein: Accel Gel, Endless edge, Hammer Gel, EFS Liquid Shot, Gu Roctane

Added caffeine: GU (most flavors), Gu Rocktane (most flavors), Clif Shot Gel (Mocha, Double Espresso, Choclate Cherry, Citrus, Strawberry); Carb-BOOM Chocolate Cherry, Hammer Gel Espresso, PowerBar Gel Double Latte, Tangerine, Chocolate, Green Apple and Strawberry-banana; Honey Stinger Ginsting and Strawberry

Added extras: EAS Energy Gel (taurine)

ENDURANCE FOOD
Jelly Belly Sports Beans. Clif Shot Bloks, Carb BOOM! Energy Chews, Sharkies, SPIZ. FRS Healthy Energy Chews

RECOVERY DRINKS (Carbs with a little protein)
Amino Vital, First Endurance Ultragen, EAS Endurathon, Perpetuem, PowerBar Recovery Drinks, Recoverite, Go Energy Drink, Endurox R4, Gatorade Nutrition Shake, Hormel's Great Shake, GNC's Distance, Clif Shot Recovery Drink. First Endurance Ultragen, Gu Brew Recovery,

ENERGY DRINKS: (Concentrated sugar, often with added caffeine):
Red Bull, Rock Star, Monster, Rebound-fx, Full Throttle

ENERGY BARS *(should be eaten for extra energy, not for a meal replacement):*
All natural/organic ((have no added vitamins or minerals):
Clif Nectar, Clif Mojo, Lara Bar, Optimum, TrailMix HoneyBar, Odwalla Bar, PowerBar Nut Naturals, KIND Bars, Zing Bars, NRG-Bar, Honey Stinger Bars, Kashi Bars, Peak Energy, Perfect 10, Gnu Bar, Raw Revolution Bar, Olympic Granola Bar, Pure Bar, Pro bar, Sun Valley Bar

Caffeine-containing bar: Peak Energy Plus

Grocery store bars: Nature Valley Granola Bar, Quaker Chewy Bars, Nutri-Grain Bar, Fig Newtons

Dairy-free: Clif Nectar, Pure Fit, Perfect 10, Larabar, Clif Builder's Bar, AllerEnergy Bar, Soy Rocks Bar, Olympic Granola Bar

Fructose-free: JayBar

Gluten-free: Larabar, Perfect 10, Elev8Me, Hammer Bar, EnvirKids Rice Cereal Bar; Omega Smart Bars, Extend Bar, Zing Bar, BoraBora Bar, Wings of Nature Bar

Wheat-free: Clif Nectar, Odwalla, Clif Builder

Kosher: Pure Fit, Larabar, Extend Bar, Balance Bar

Meal replacement bar *(offers 10-15 g protein, fiber, some fat, vitamins, minerals-but not enough calories for a whole meal):*
Kashi Go Lean Bar , Balance Satisfaction, MetRx Mr. Big, MET-Rx Big 100 Colossal

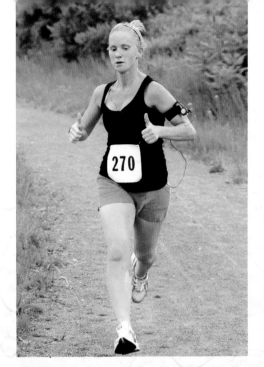

Nut-free: AllerEnergy Bars, Metaballs

Peanut-free: Soy Rocks, AllerEnergy bar, Larabar (has other nuts)

Protein bars *(Your choice of soy, whey, egg, or blended protein source):*
PowerBar ProteinPlus, EAS Myoplex Delux, High 5 Protein Bar, Maximuscle Promax Meal, USN Pure Protein, Atkins Advantage, Tri-O-Plex, Clif Builder's Bar, Detour Bar, Honey Stinger Protein Bar

Raw food: Raw Revolution, Pure Bar

Recovery bar (4:1 carb:pro ratio): PowerBar Performance

Soy-free: Larabar, Perfect 10 Natural Energy, Clif Nectar, KIND Bar, Bumble Bar, NRG-Bar, AllerEnergy Bar, Zing Bar

Vegan: Pure Fit, Lara Bar, Hammer Bar, Vega Whole Food Raw Energy Bar, Clif Builder's Bar, Perfect 10, Soy Rocks Bars

Vitamin & protein-pumped candy bar: Marathon Bar; Detour Bar

Women's bars (fewer calories; soy, calcium, iron and folic acid):
PowerBar Pria, Amino Vital Fit, Luna Bar, Balance Oasis

40-30-30 Bars: Balance Bar, ZonePerfect

- four 8-ounce glasses of sports drink and a banana
- two 8-ounce glasses of sports drink plus an energy bar (plus extra water)
- five fig cookies plus water

This is more calories than many marathoners voluntarily consume during long runs or walks. Hence, you need to practiced *programmed* eating and drinking. Then, on marathon day, you will know:

- what and how much you can tolerate
- how you can comfortably carry the sports snacks.

Fanny packs or running shorts with multiple pockets are a good way to carry your snacks. Some marathoners set the timer on their watch to go off every 30 to 45 minutes, to ensure they'll eat on a schedule. You might also want to have friends meet you at designated areas along the course. Also check the marathon's website to find out what snacks they will offer along the route. But always carry some back-up fuel with you 1) in case you miss seeing your friends or 2) the snack table runs out of gels or has only the yucky flavored gels remaining.

Whatever you do, think ahead and make a clear plan before marathon day. You must also be flexible. Who knows what happens when your body is pushed to the limit. Even tried-and-true favorites can become unpalatable.

Fuel Suggestions

Whereas the fastest runners are able to do well with just carbohydrate-containing fluids, slower runners and walkers, who are going to be on the marathon course longer, will likely do better with not only fluids but also solids that provide more calories and also a flavor change. (Just how many hours in a row can you consume sports drinks and gels without getting "sugared-out"?) There is no magic to the special sports foods (e.g., gels, sports beans, energy bars) that are available at your local running store. These engineered foods are simply pre-wrapped and convenient, use them if you prefer, but also know you could save money—and add pleasure—by fueling with sugar cookies and twizzlers.

The carbs you consume during the marathon will also keep you in good spirits. Some runners become moody, irritable, and irrational towards the end of a marathon. Running partners can become either the best of friends or the worst of enemies.

> " For the walkers and slower runners who will be out for 6 or more hours, I recommend peanut-butter-and-honey sandwiches, just like mom made when you were a kid. Make them up the night before so the bread really soaks up the honey. "
>
> *Earl Fenstermacher,*
> *Seattle, WA*

Undesired Pit Stops

Many marathoners fear that fluids or foods taken during the event will cause diarrhea. Diarrhea commonly occurs in novice runners, whose intestinal tracts are not fully adjusted to the jostling of 26.2 miles. With experience, the problem tends to abate, but even some experienced runners carry toilet paper with them! If you fear diarrhea attacks, experiment during training with dietary changes to see if less fiber (such as in bran cereals, whole grains, fruits and vegetables) can reduce the problem. Or try less milk (switch to lactose-free milk products). Some athletes simply need to abstain from food for three or four hours pre-event.

Diarrhea is also common among marathoners who lose more than 4 percent of their body weight during the race (6 pounds for a 150-pound person; 3 kg/70 kg). Hence, the fluids you drink may actually help prevent diarrhea, not cause it. I once talked to a runner who tried to abstain from consuming anything—even water—during a marathon in fear it would upset his stomach. He held off as long as he could without fluids. Then when he did succumb, he got diarrhea. Although he blamed the diarrhea on the drink, I tend to think the lack of prior fluid intake was the bigger problem.

> " Because I am a slow runner, I would typically get hungry during a long run and my energy level would plummet. I would try eating yet-another sweet sports bar, which is full of carbohydrates, but it did very little to help; I had already had my fill of carbs. I realized that my body was craving something more solid; so I switched to a sports bar that has more protein. That has made all the difference.
>
> Brenda Van Oosten,
> Brecksville, OH
>
> "

The Gastric Bypass Marathoner

About 6% of people who have had gastric bypass surgery become endurance athletes. They may start walking as a part of their weight reduction program, and then end up setting a goal to complete a marathon. Exercise takes on a bigger purpose and becomes more than just "burning off calories."

Because people who have had bypass surgery have very small stomachs, they cannot eat much food nor can they drink large volumes of fluid. They often get into trouble with dehydration and low blood sugar during long walks or runs. They commonly experience intestinal distress if they digest sugary foods such as gels, sports drinks, and gummy candy.

If you have had bypass surgery, you need to experiment with fueling your body for long distances. Redefine food as fuel (not as fattening) and mechanically eat and drink small amounts, such as one jellybean every 10 minutes. Learn your sweat rate and continually take small sips of water, trying to match what you lose, if at all possible.

By partnering with a sports dietitian, you can develop a fueling program that will keep you out of the medical tents. To find a local sports RD, go to www.SCANdpg.org.

Summary

Preventing dehydration and low blood sugar is crucial to a successful marathon. The fluids and foods that you consume during your long walks or runs should be an extension of your carbohydrate-rich daily training diet. Because each marathoner has individual tolerances and preferences, you'll want to learn—by trial and error during training—what foods and fluids settle best and contribute to top competitive performance. Don't ruin months of physical training—and your marathon—with poor nutritional training.

Cheesecake Snackwich

While real cheesecake is a great way to fat-load, this snackwich is a smart way to enjoy a few carbs before you run. The snackwich uses graham crackers, an easy-to-digest pre-run snack. Graham crackers as a tasty way to enjoy whole grains and you can make them even yummier by adding a dab of lowfat cream cheese and jam or honey.

Pan ahead: make a make a bunch of these snackwiches and freeze them, so they will be ready and waiting for a pre-run energy fix. Frozen, they taste remarkably like an ice cream sandwich!

Yield: 1 serving

2 graham cracker squares
1 teaspoon cream cheese, preferably lowfat
1 teaspoon jam, fruit spread, or honey

Optional: sprinkling of cinnamon.

1. Spread one graham cracker with lowfat cream cheese.
2. Add the jam and then sprinkle with cinnamon, if desired.
3. Top with the second graham cracker, making it into a sandwich.

Calories per serving: 90

Carbohydrate 16 g
Protein 2 g
Fat 2 g

Chapter 11

Recovering from Exhaustive Training

You haven't finished training until you have refueled! That's right; refueling after you finish an exhausting walk or run is just as important as fueling beforehand. Rapid refueling optimizes recovery and can reduce muscle soreness. So before you dash off to a post-workout obligation (school, work, meeting, etc.), be sure to eat; eating anything is better than nothing, even if you have to gobble the food on the run! By refueling your muscles after hard workouts, you can better endure repeated days—and months—of marathon training.

While your recovery diet after hard workouts (long runs, speed workouts, hill workouts) is important, on easy days you have less glycogen depletion and less muscle damage. Hence, immediate refueling is less critical but never the less, a good habit to maintain. If nothing else, a recovery snack can curb your appetite and help with weight management.

Proper recovery diets are particularly important for marathoners who do double workouts (such as run in the morning, then lift weights in the afternoon) or for weekend warriors (who do their long run, then ski the rest of the day with their family). They need to rapidly refuel because they are exercising within six hours. They don't have time to waste; their muscles need fuel as soon as tolerable post-exercise to prepare for the soon-to-come second workout.

Perhaps you are wondering what you should eat to hasten recovery? Here are the answers to questions marathoners commonly ask about recovery foods.

What is the Best Recovery Food Plan?

During a hard workout, you damage your muscles with tiny injuries and deplete your muscles of glycogen. Hence, afterwards, you should optimize recovery by consuming a little protein to repair the muscle damage and adequate carbs to refuel the depleted glycogen stores. You don't need to eat tons of food—about 200 to 400 calories (50 to 100 g; 0.5 to 0.75 g carb/lb; 1.0-1.5 g carb/kg) of carbohydrate-based foods along with about 10 grams of protein within an hour after hard exercise. Then repeat this dose every 1 to 2 hours for five or six hours. Most marathoners tend to naturally follow this grazing pattern with repeated snacks and meals, assuming they are not "dieting" or "too busy" to eat.

Good carb + protein recovery choices include:
• fruit yogurt
• chocolate milk
• cereal with milk
• turkey on a bulkie roll
• chicken dinner with rice and vegetables
• spaghetti with meat sauce.

If you are on the road, carry with you:
• trail mix (nuts and raisins)
• bagel with peanut butter

- Go-gurt (liquid yogurt)
- Energy bar with 3 to 4 times as many carbs as protein.

Some marathoners like commercial recovery drinks, like Accelerade or Endurox. Others inappropriately choose protein shakes that lack the carbs needed to replace depleted glycogen stores. Just remember: engineered foods lack all the health-protective nutrients that you get in "real food," so be sure to balance them into an overall healthful diet.

> When I come back from a long, hard training run, I'm generally exhausted and in need of some quick energy. I've been known to drink maple syrup right from the bottle. Tastes great!
>
> *Bill Rodgers,*
> *Boston, MA*

What if I'm Not Hungry after a Run?

If you get hot and sweaty during a long run, you might not feel hungry right away. But sooner or later, when your body temperature returns to normal, you will get hungry. After all, you burn about 1,000 calories or more during a 10 miler and your body needs to replace that fuel! The sooner you refuel, the sooner your muscles have the tools (protein and carbs) they need to recover— and the sooner you will feel better. So rather than "hold off" until you feel hungry, at least quench your thirst by drinking some fluids—preferably chocolate milk (for carbs and protein). If not chocolate milk, then juices or sports drinks.

If even the thought of post-exercise food or fluids makes you nauseated, you likely had a very tough workout. After a 20+ mile training run or the marathon itself, many marathoners have no interest in putting anything in their stomachs! In such a case, try to consume a little ginger ale, chicken noodle soup, watermelon or other watery food that appeals to you and offers a few carbs and some fluid. But the reality is you need not rapidly refuel because you will be taking a rest day the next day. Your muscles will have time to refuel and recover before your next workout. Yet, rapid refueling does reduce muscle soreness. For that reason alone, try to eat or drink as soon as tolerable.

How Much Should I Drink?

You should replace fluid losses as soon as possible to help your body restore normal water balance. If you weigh yourself pre- and post-exercise, you'll know exactly how much you dehydrate, how much you need to drink to rehydrate—and how much you should drink during long runs to prevent the deficit in the first place. That is, if you started your run at 130 pounds and ended at 128 pounds, you lost 2 pounds (32 ounces, 1 quart) of sweat. Rehydrate with 1 quart (2 lbs), if not 50% more. And during your next training session on that route, plan to drink an additional quart of fluid.

> At the end of each long walk, I have found that I recover much more quickly if I sip on orange juice and eat at least half a banana.
>
> *Shelley Smith,*
> *Highlands Ranch, CO*

Throughout the day, keep a water bottle on your desk, in your car, or in your backpack, so you'll easily be able to drink enough to quench your thirst. Sometimes, you may not feel thirsty, but your body can need more fluids. You'll know that you are well hydrated when you are urinating every 2 to 4 hours and have pale-colored urine. Refer to chapter 8 for a urine color chart and more information.

What Should I Drink?

Here are some popular fluid options, and how to balance them into your sports diet:

- *Plain water.* Water provides only water but not the carbohydrates you need to replenish depleted muscle glycogen nor the protein you need to repair and build muscles. Consume carb-protein foods along with the water, such as a bagel with peanut butter, apple with cheese, or energy bar (with both carbs and protein). For sodium (enhances fluid retention), snack on some salty foods (baked chips, pretzels, pizza) along with the plain water (or any beverage, for that matter).

- *Chocolate milk.* Milk is an excellent source of high quality protein to repair muscles, as well as calcium, riboflavin and an array of life-sustaining nutrients. The flavoring (chocolate—or vanilla, strawberry, or coffee) offers carbs (sugar) to refuel muscles. If you are lactose intolerant or prefer to not drink dairy, then flavored lactose-free milks or flavored soy milk are fine alternatives.

- *Soft drinks.* Colas, in particular, are popular recovery fluids. Granted, soft drinks lack nutritional value and are filled with empty calories, but they do offer both carbohydrates and fluids. Most colas also offer caffeine, which for some runners provides welcome stimulation. Historically, marathoners have been told to avoid caffeine because of a supposed diuretic effect. Newer research indicates caffeine is not dehydrating and is unlikely to hinder recovery.

- *Juices.* Fruit and vegetable juices are always an excellent choice because they not only offer a rich supply of carbohydrates, they also offer the vitamin C your body needs to optimize healing. Fruit smoothies, made by blending orange juice with a banana and some yogurt, create a powerful recovery drink!

- *Sports drinks.* Commercial fluid replacers are designed to be used during exercise; they are dilute and easy to digest. They provide fewer recovery carbohydrates than juices or soft drinks. That is, 8 ounces of a commercial fluid replacer offers half the carbohydrates of 8 ounces of most juices. Sports drinks are a fair source of carbs, and a poor source of vitamins. They offer a little sodium but far less than you'd get from a few crackers or a recovery meal.

- *Commercial recovery drinks.* Some recovery drinks (such as Endurox, Accelerade) come with a little protein added; those might be better than drinks with only carbs (Gatorade, PowerAde). These commercial beverages are convenient, but they offer nothing that cannot be found in standard foods. In fact, they offer less; they lack the nutritional power of a multitude of vitamins and phytochemicals found in wholesome foods. While there is a time and a place for convenience, in the long run you'll be better off refueling yourself primarily with real foods that are less processed and more nutritionally complete than a commercial carb-protein-vitamin formula. I encourage my clients to enjoy fruit smoothies or chocolate milk.

Do I Need Extra Protein?

While eating a little protein along with recovery carbohydrates is a smart choice, you do not need to "protein load" and eat a protein-based recovery diet. That is, do not choose a protein bar or protein shake for your recovery food unless is has three or four times more carbs than protein. (Read the food label to determine the carb and protein content of the product.)

At recovery meals, if you fill up on a cheese omelet, steak, or chicken Caesar salad, you'll miss out on the carbohydrate-rich bagel, potato, and bread that you need to refuel depleted glycogen stores. In general, most marathoners can meet their protein needs with:

- a serving of protein-rich food at two meals a day (such as turkey on sandwich at lunch and lean hamburger in spaghetti sauce at dinner)
- a serving of dairy food at each meal (such as lowfat milk on cereal, a yogurt at lunch, and (lowfat) cheese with crackers before dinner; soy alternatives are fine). Refer to chapter 6 for more information.

Many marathoners report craving protein after hard exercise. If that's the case for you, eat the burger, and be sure

Popular Recovery Foods

Your muscles are most receptive to replacing depleted glycogen stores immediately after exercise. By feeding them carbohydrates, preferably with a little bit of protein, you can optimize the recovery process. Don't get hung-up on the recommended 4 to 1 ratio of carbs to protein. Simply fill-up on carbs more so than protein.

If you can't tolerate solid foods immediately following a hard run or marathon, simply drink carbohydrate-rich fluids and/or eat watery foods, building up to mini-meals or snacks. Target 60 to 90 grams (240 to 360 calories) of carbs every two hours or so after a hard workout or long run.

Some popular choices include:

Fluids (8 oz; 240 ml):	Carb (g)	Protein (g)
Gatorade	14	--
Coke	26	--
Cranberry Juice	43	--
Accelerade	14	3
Chocolate milk	26	8
Yogurt, flavored	40	10

Solids:		
Trail mix	40	10
(raisins, granola, nuts)		
PowerBar, chocolate	45	10
Cheerios w/ milk	50	12
Pasta, 2 cups + meat sauce	100	20

to also eat the roll and other carbohydrate-rich foods as an accompaniment. This balance will help you rebuild and refuel, as well as enjoy the recovery process.

Do I Need Extra Salt to Replace what I Lose in Sweat?

In most cases, marathoners can replace more than enough salt by eating standard foods after exercise. Both walkers and runners lose some sodium (a part of salt) in sweat but are unlikely to deplete their body stores, even during a marathon. As I mentioned in chapter 8, during three hours of sweaty exercise, you might lose about 1,800 to 5,600 milligrams of sodium. Because the average 150-pound person's body contains about 97,000 milligrams of sodium, this 2 to 6 percent loss is relatively insignificant.

My favorite recovery foods are a handful of salted, dry roasted peanuts and a stack of Fig Newtons.

Earl Fernstermacher, Seattle, WA

But there are exceptions to every rule. Some marathoners are sweating for 6 hours—and have twice that loss. Others are salty sweaters and end up with a crusty layer of salt on their body. If this sounds familiar, you'll likely crave salt. In such case, you should respond appropriately by eating salty foods such as salted pretzels, soups, crackers and/or baked potatoes or other foods sprinkled with salt.

Athletes who may need extra salt include:
- slower marathoners who exercise continuously for more than four to six hours
- people who train in cold weather yet run a marathon in warm weather. This sometimes happens, for example, with Boston Marathoners if they train throughout the winter but compete on what turns out to be an unusually warm spring day. It also happens with people who live in cold climates, like Minnesota, but run a marathon where the weather is hot, such as Hawaii.
- marathoners who drink only water (as opposed to a sodium-containing sports drink) during extended runs or walks.

Recovering from the Marathon

Some runners and walkers are all smiles after crossing the finish line. Others feel nauseous, achy, and horrid. Hopefully, you will have consumed the optimal combination of water, carbs, and sodium during the marathon to put you into the "exhilarated" category. But if you are feeling nauseous, try sipping on ginger ale or cola. Some salty, brothy chicken noodle soup might taste good, as might a few saltines or pretzels. The sooner you can get fluids, carbs, and sodium into your system, the better you will start to feel.

Many marathoners who are ready to celebrate participate in a post-marathon dinner with wine, cheese, steak, ice cream, and other high fat, low carb foods that might not have been a part of their training diet. That's OK, because they will have plenty of time after the marathon to replace depleted glycogen stores and can be less strict with choosing recovery carbohydrates (as discussed at the beginning of this chapter). Go with what you want and perhaps crave. For some, that's potato chips, for others it's a thick steak.

Yes, you do want to continue to eat:
- plenty of post-marathon recovery carbohydrates to refuel your muscles
- adequate protein (to help with healing damaged muscles)
- salty foods to replace electrolyte losses
- nutrient-dense fruits and vegetables to optimize health.

But you need not be obsessive with your recovery diet because you will not be demanding much from your muscles for a while.

If you choose to celebrate with beer, wine, or Champagne, be sure to eat something (anything!) first so that you are not drinking alcohol on an empty stomach, and also drink some juice or soft drinks for fluids and carbohydrates.

Surprisingly, you might even have energy to enjoy the post-marathon dance party if you eat well. A nice massage and a gentle swim or bike ride to loosen stiff muscles without pounding the joints are also welcomed suggestions that enhance blood flow to your muscles to help them get needed nutrients and carry away waste products.

Plan plenty of time to heal damaged muscles. The standard recommendation is to allow a rest day from running for every mile you ran—that's 26 days of recovery (or cross-training). If you are fearful you'll gain weight without running mega-miles, relax. You won't (unless you really indulge). Rest is an essential part of your training program. If you feel compelled to run to "burn off calories," keep reading, the section on Weight Management (chapters 14, 15, and 16) might help you relax.

Summary

You haven't finished your training until you have refueled! On a daily basis, plan time to refuel with nutrient-dense foods and fluids. Proper refueling will help you feel more energetic the rest of the day. Choosing carb-based foods with a little protein will enhance recovery and reduce post-exercise muscle soreness.
After a marathon, you will not be doing any hard exercise for several days, so you need not be obsessed with refueling rapidly. Yet, the sooner you consume carbs, water, sodium, and protein, the sooner you will feel better and want to celebrate your awesome accomplishment.

Strawberry Banana Smoothie

Smoothies are good for a light meal or post-run recovery drink. They both quench your thirst and satisfy your appetite. Plus, they are an easy way to boost your fruit intake

Be creative when you make smoothies. Just about any combination of milk, juice or yogurt plus fruit will taste great. By keeping your freezer filled with sliced peaches, banana chunks, strawberries and blueberries, you'll be ready to whip up a tasty treat.

If you make this recipe with strawberry yogurt (as opposed to strawberry-banana yogurt), add one whole banana rather than half. Using frozen fruit makes a thicker and frostier shake.

Blend together:
1 6-ounce (180 g) container strawberry banana yogurt
6 ounces (180 ml) cranberry juice
4 strawberries, preferably frozen
1/2 banana, preferably in chunks that have been peeled and frozen
4 ice cubes
1/4 cup (35 g) powdered milk or protein powder

Yield: 1 satisfying meal-in-a-glass
Total Calories: 450
Calories per serving: 450

90 g Carbohydrate
19 g Protein
1 g Fat

Recipe courtesy of Cori Alexander. Reprinted with permission: *Food Guide for Soccer: Tips and Recipes from the Pros* by Gloria Averbuch and Nancy Clark.

Chapter 12

Marathon Week: Nutrition Preparations

Seven days and counting down to the marathon. I'll bet you are getting a bit anxious? The good news is you need not worry about running out of energy and hitting the wall if you have done a good job of practicing your fueling before, during, and after your long runs. Although 26.2 miles is, indeed, a very long distance to walk or run, optimal fueling will make a big difference in your ability to not only finish the marathon but also enjoy it.

For some marathoners, the enjoyment starts with carbohydrate-loading at the pre-marathon pasta party. Yet, carbo-loading means more than just stuffing yourself with pasta. Here's some food for thought.

> **"** During one of our training meetings, we prepare an 'energy food buffet.' The other coach and I bring a variety of energy bars, gels, and sports drinks. We cut, squirt, and pour so that our marathoners can taste a variety of flavors and textures. By having our buffet, people can sample a wide variety of products. They can then purchase what they think might work for them and try those on their training runs. We constantly remind them: Don't use it in the race if you haven't trained with it!
>
> *Chris Davis, Joints in Motion coach, Duluth, MN* **"**

Pre-marathon Training Diet

You can't simply eat a big dinner of pasta the night before the marathon and expect to run well. Your muscles have to be receptive to storing the carbohydrates, and that naturally happens as a response to your months of training.

To support the rigors of marathon training, you should have been eating a carbohydrate-rich sports diet *every* day as the foundation for *every* meal. Runners and walkers who carbohydrate-based diet every day (i.e., 55 to 65 percent of the calories from carbohydrates) can train better because their muscles are better fueled. Plus, they can develop a tried-and-true training diet that will support 26.2 miles of marathoning.

The last thing you want to do is change your diet before the marathon. To avoid nutritional mistakes on marathon day, *during training* you should:
- Practice eating your planned pre-marathon breakfast. If you will be traveling a long distance to the marathon, be sure this tried-and-true food will be available on marathon day.
- Start some of your long training runs and walks at the time you'll be running or walking on marathon day. For example, if your marathon starts at 10:00 a.m., do some training runs that start at 10:00 a.m. The Disney Marathon in Orlando starts at 6:00 a.m., so do some early morning runs.
- Learn how much pre-exercise food you can eat and then comfortably run or walk.
- Practice drinking the sports drink that will be available on race day as well as any mid-run foods (gels, fruit) you plan to eat. (Visit the marathon's website to learn what products will be available and at which mile mark you can expect them.)

These nutrition preparations will help reduce surprises!

The Week Before the Marathon

The biggest change in your schedule during the week before your marathon should be in your *training*, not in your food. You'll want to taper off your training so that your muscles have the opportunity to become fully fueled. Don't bother with any last-minute hard training that will burn off carbohydrates rather than allow them to be stored. Instead, for a Sunday marathon, limit yourself to four miles on Monday and Tuesday, rest on Wednesday, three on Thursday, rest on Friday (travel day) and Saturday (light sightseeing).

You need not eat hundreds more calories this week. You simply need to exercise less. This way, the 600 to 1,000 calories you generally expend during training can be used to fuel your muscles. All during this week, you should maintain your tried-and-true carbohydrate-based training diet. Drastic changes commonly lead to upset stomachs, diarrhea, or constipation. For example, carbo-loading on an unusually high amount of fruits and juices might cause diarrhea. Too many white-flour, low-fiber bagels, breads, and pasta might clog your system.

Be sure that you are *carbo*-loading, not *fat*-loading. Some runners eat two pats of butter per dinner roll, big dollops of sour cream on a potato, and enough dressing to drown a salad. These fatty foods fill the stomach and the fat cells but leave the muscles less fueled. Your best bet is to trade the extra fats for extra carbohydrates:

- Instead of having one roll with butter for 200 calories, have two plain rolls for 200 calories.
- Have pasta with tomato sauce or lowfat sauces rather than oil-based or cheese-based toppings.
- Enjoy lowfat frozen yogurt instead of gourmet ice cream.

Many marathoners totally avoid protein-rich foods the days before the marathon. This is unnecessary because your body still needs protein on a daily basis. Endurance runners even burn a little protein for energy. Hence, you can and should eat a small serving of lowfat proteins such as poached eggs, yogurt, turkey, or chicken as the *accompaniment* to the meal (not the main focus), or plant proteins such as beans and lentils (if your intestines can tolerate them).

The Day Before the Marathon

By now, you may have gained about three to four pounds, but don't panic. This weight gain reflects *water weight*. For every ounce of carbohydrate stored in your body, you store about three ounces of water. You can tell if your muscles are well saturated with carbohydrates if the scale has gone up a few pounds.

Instead of relying upon a huge pasta dinner the night before the marathon, you might want to enjoy a substantial carbo-feast at breakfast or lunch. This earlier

 There's more to preparing for the marathon than just eating carbs. The marathon is a mind game. You have to program your mind in order to do it.

Hal Gabriel, Newton MA

Tools for Carbo-loading

When carbo-loading, you want to consume about 3 to 5 grams carbohydrates per pound of body weight (6 to 10 g/kg).

Divide your target grams of carbohydrates into three parts of the day:
breakfast + snack   (7:00 am to noon)
lunch + snack   (noon to 5:00 pm)
dinner + snack   (5:00 to 10:00 pm)

Choose foods to hit your target! You can find carbohydrate info on food labels and websites such as www.fitday.com or www.calorieking.com

If you weigh:	Total #g carb/day	Target #g carbs per five hours: 7:00 a.m.-noon; noon-5:00 pm; 5:00-10:00 pm
100 lbs (45 kg)	300 to 500 g	100 to 175 g
125 lbs (57 kg)	375 to 625 g	125 to 210 g
150 lbs (68 kg)	450 to 750 g	150 to 250 g
175 lbs (80 kg)	525 to 875 g	175 to 290 g

Sample 50 gram carbohydrate choices for the foundation of a meal or snack
- Wheaties, 2 cups (60 g)
- Nature Valley Granola Bar, 2 packets (4 bars; 3 oz; 84 g)
- Thomas' Bagel, 1 (3.5 oz; 100 g)
- Banana, 2 medium (8 oz; 225 g)
- Orange juice, 16 ounces (480 ml)
- Apple, 2 medium (10 oz; 280 g)
- Raisins, 1/2 cup (70 g)
- Pepperidge Farm multi-grain bread, 2.5 slices (75 g)
- Baked potato, 1 large (6.5 ounces; 180 g)
- Pasta, 1 cup cooked (140 g)
- Rice, 1 cup cooked (160 g)
- Fig Newtons, 5 (2.5 oz; 75 g)
- Flavored Yogurt (1 cup; 230 g) + 3 graham cracker squares

meal allows plenty of time for the food to move through your system. Or, eat at both times!

You'll be better off eating a little bit too much than too little on the eve of the marathon. But you don't want to overeat either. Learning the right balance takes practice. Let each preparatory race and long run be opportunities to learn.

> I never eat a very big meal the night before a marathon, as it usually gives me trouble the next day. I prefer to eat a bigger lunch, then a lighter supper.
>
> *Grete Waitz, Norway*

Be sure to drink extra water, juices, and even carbohydrate-rich soft drinks, if desired. Abstain from too much wine, beer, and alcoholic beverages. While one glass of wine or a can of beer may be OK—particularly if you if you consume it along with a carb-based meal and water, two or three drinks can hurt your ability to perform well the next day. Your best bet it to be well saturated with water, not hung-over with alcohol.

Marathon Morning

With luck, you'll wake up to a clear, crisp day that makes you want to jump out of bed and walk or run! Before embarking upon your day's task, be sure to eat breakfast. One of the biggest nutritional mistakes made by novice marathoners is eating too little beforehand, fearing that eating will result in an upset stomach.

As I've repeatedly mentioned, be sure to eat pre-marathon foods that are tried-and-true. That is, don't feast on a pancake breakfast marathon morning only to discover that pancakes settle like a lead brick. Some marathoners can eat a bagel, juice, or about 500 calories of a breakfast one to three hours before the event; many carry familiar foods with them to the pre-race "athletes' village." Others want more time for their stomach to empty; they've learned they run best if they wake up at 4 a.m., eat a bowl of oatmeal, and then go back to bed.

Here are some examples of simple 500-calorie pre-marathon breakfasts. You might want more (or fewer) calories, depending on your body size and tolerance to food:

Oatmeal, 2 packets made with	300 calories
Milk, 1 cup lowfat (240 ml)	100
Banana, medium	100
Bagel (Dunkin Donuts)	300
Peanut butter, 2 Tbsp (30 g)	200
PowerBar, 1	230
Yogurt, flavored	250
Gatorade, 8 oz. (240 ml)	50
Eggs, 2 poached on	150
Toast, 2 slices	200
Orange juice, 12 oz. (360 ml)	150

Two Sample Carbo-loading Food Plans (3,200-3,400 Calories)

These menus are appropriate for a 150 pound (68 kg) athlete who needs about 4 grams carb per pound body weight (8 g/kg) to adequately carbo-load.

	Approximate Calories	Carbs (g)
Wheaties, 2 cups (60 g)	220	48
Milk, 1% lowfat, 8 ounces (240 ml)	100	12
Bagel, 1 (3.5 ounce; 100 g)	300	55
Honey, 1 Tbsp (20 g)	60	17
Orange juice, 12 ounces (360 ml)	160	40
Breakfast: 830 cals, 75% carb		
Whole grain bread, 2 slices (60 g)	200	40
Peanut butter, 2 Tbsp (30 g)	200	8
Jelly, 2 Tbsp (30 g)	100	25
Fruit yogurt, 8 oz. (240 ml)	230	35
Pretzels, 2 oz (60 g)	230	48
Lunch: 970 cals, 65% carb		
Apple, 1 large (7 oz; 120 g)	120	30
Graham crackers, 4 squares	120	22
Snack total: 240 cals; 90% car		
Chicken breast, 5 oz (140 g)	250	—
Rice, 1.5 cups cooked (240 g)	300	65
Brocolli, 1 cup (180 g)	50	10
Dinner rolls, 2 whole wheat (2 oz; 60 g)	200	40
Dinner: 800 cals; 60% carb		
Banana, 1 medium (4 oz; 120 g)	100	24
Sherbert, 1 cup; (240 ml)	260	45
PM snack: 360 cals, ~100% carb		
TOTAL Menu #1	3,200	547 g
~70% carb; ~4 g carb/lb for a 150 lb athlete		

Menu #2

Oatmeal, 1 cup dry (3 oz; 85 g), cooked in	300	55
Milk, 16 ounces (480 ml)	200	25
Raisins, 1/4 cup (35 g)	130	30
Brown sugar, 1.5 Tbsp (15 g)	50	12
Apple juice, 8 oz. (240 ml)	120	30
Breakfast: 800 cals; 75% carb		
Sub sandwich roll, 6" (4 oz; 110 g)	320	60
Lean meat (4 oz; 110 g)	200	—
Fruit yogurt, 8 oz (240 ml)	240	40
Grape juice, 12 oz (360 ml)	220	55
Lunch: 980 cals; 80% carb		
Fig Newtons, 6	330	65
Banana large (6 oz; 180 g)	150	36
Snack: 480 cals; 85% carb		
Spaghetti, 2 cups cooked (280 g)	400	80
Prego spaghetti sauce, 1 cup (250 g)	250	40
Italian bread, 2 slices (1.5 oz; 45 g)	150	30
Root beer, 12 ounces (360 ml)	140	38
Dinner: 940 cals; 80% carb		
Canned peaches in syrup, 1 cup (260 g)	200	48
Snack: 200 cals; ~100% carb		
TOTAL Menu #2	**3,400**	**644 g**

   ~75% carb; ~4.5 g carb/lb for a 150 lb athlete

> **I drink coffee before a marathon, just like I drink coffee every day. It's a part of my normal routine. I like coffee not because it boosts my energy but rather because it helps me go to the bathroom.**
>
> *Bill Rodgers, Boston, MA*

Drink plenty of fluids on marathon morning. Water and sports drinks are popular choices. Some runners drink coffee for stimulation or for its laxative effect. Others prefer to abstain from coffee because they are already nervous and jittery and have no need for an added buzz. Choose what's best for your body—do what you would normally do before your long training runs. If you are traveling, you need to have planned ahead! (See Chapter 13.)

Whatever beverage you like to drink, take it with you in a throw-away bottle so you'll have it available at the race.

Because water takes about 45 to 90 minutes to move through your system, you can drink several glasses up to two hours before the marathon, have time to urinate the excess, then tank up again 5 to 15 minutes before the starting gun. With pre-race nerves, don't be surprised if you are urinating twenty times!

Fueling During the Marathon

Your job during the marathon is to prevent dehydration and to maintain a normal blood sugar level. I have discussed those topics in chapters 8, 9, and 10. Remember, you should be doing nothing new, special, or different during the marathon. Stick with what has worked for you in your training runs. That is, stick with the tried-and-true.

Summary

By marathon day, you should be well trained. You should have not only strong muscles but also a strong knowledge of the foods and fluids you need to fuel those muscles. Knowing you are nutritionally prepared, you need not fear that you will tire prematurely or "hit the wall." Instead, you can focus on the day's job—to enjoy the 26.2 miles with energy to spare!

Easy Lasagna

This recipe is "easy" because it eliminates the step of cooking the lasagna noodles before assembly.

When eating this lasagna pre-event, be aware that almost half the calories come from protein and fat. (Most lasagnas are even higher in protein and fat!) Be sure to round out the meal with (whole grain) rolls, fruit salad, juice and other carbohydrate-rich foods.

1 pound (2 cups; 500 g) part-skim ricotta or cottage cheese or a mixture
1 egg or substitute
1 teaspoon (1.5 g) dried oregano
1 teaspoon (5 g) salt, as desired
1 48-ounce (1,345 g) jar spaghetti sauce
2 cups (480 ml) water
20 lasagna noodles (a one-pound (450 g) box has 24 noodles)
4 to 6 ounces (1 to 1 1/2 cups; 120 to 180 g) mozarella cheese, shredded

Optional: Your choice of –
1 10-ounce (300 g) package frozen chopped spinach, thawed and drained
4 cups (1 liter) diced vegetables (onions, mushrooms. carrots, zucchini, summer squash, etc.) steamed or sauted in a little oil
1 pound (450 g) extra-lean hamburger or ground turkey, browned and drained
1 pound (450 g) tofu, crumbled

1. In a bowl, mix the ricotta cheese with the egg, spinach, oregano, salt (and vegetables and meat).
2. In a 9jx 13" lasagna pan (23 x 38 cm), place some sauce, then a layer of 4 uncooked lasagna noodles. Add a layer of cheese/vegetable mixture, then spaghetti sauce. Repeat three times, ending with noodles. Sprinkle shredded mozarella over the top.
3. Pour the 2 cups of water around the edges. Cover tightly with foil and bake at 350°F (175°C) for about 1 hour and 15 minutes, uncovering for the last 10 minutes. (Try to prevent the foil from sticking to the top cheese by covering it carefully.)

Yield: 8 servings
Total calories: 3,700
Calories per serving: 460

Carbohydrates	64 grams
Protein	22 grams
Fat	13 grams

Carb-loading Menu

	calories	carbs
1 serving lasagna	460 calories	64 g carbs
French bread (2 oz; 60 g)	150	25
Fruit salad, bowl	140	35
Cranapple juice, 8 oz (240 g)	150	38

Total: 900 calories
162 g carbs (72% calories from carbohydrates)

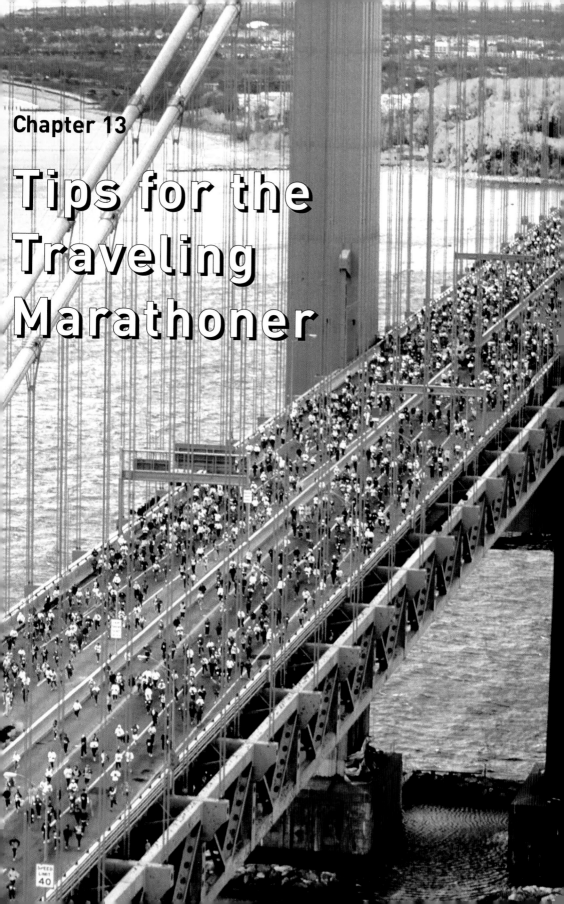

Tips for the Traveling Marathoner

Participating in a marathon that is far away from your home provides a fun excuse to travel. But once you arrive at the host location, be sure to fight the urge to do too much pre-marathon sightseeing. All too often when traveling, marathoners get sidetracked by the confusion and excitement of being in a new city. Restrain yourself and save the sightseeing until *after* the event.

Your first priority is to put your feet up, rest your legs, relax with some juice and other tried-and-true carbohydrates, and visualize yourself completing the entire marathon smoothly, strongly, and successfully. You'll also want to review how you are going to best fuel yourself. Some marathoners travel with a cooler packed with abundant tried-and-true meals and snacks. Others confront the nutritional challenges of finding familiar sports foods at local restaurants—and struggle to avoid the rich temptations that lurk in every bakery, deli, and dessert cart.

To help you better accommodate a pre-marathon high-carbohydrate sports diet into your traveling routine, use these tips.

Breakfast:
- At a restaurant, order pancakes, French toast, whole-wheat toast, or English, bran, or corn muffins. Add jelly, jam, or maple syrup for extra carbohydrates, but hold the butter or request that it be served on the side so that you can better control the amount of fat in your meal.
- Order a *large* orange juice or tomato juice. This can help compensate for a potential lack of fruits or veggies in the other meals.
- For a hotel stay, you might want to save time and money by packing your own cereal, raisins, and spoon. Either bring powdered milk or buy a chug of lowfat milk at a local convenience store. A water glass or milk carton can double as a cereal bowl.

Lunch:
- Find a deli or restaurant that offers wholesome breads. Request a sandwich that emphasizes the bread, rather than the filling (preferably lean beef, turkey, ham, or chicken). Hold the mayonnaise, and instead, add moistness with mustard or ketchup, sliced tomatoes, and lettuce. Add more carbohydrates with juice, fruit, fig bars (brought from a corner store), or yogurt for dessert.
- At fast-food restaurants, the burgers, fried fish, special sandwiches, and French fries have a very high fat content. You'll get more carbohydrates by sticking to the spaghetti, baked potatoes, chili, or thick-crust pizza selections.

Packing Your Cooler

One key to successfully selecting a top-notch sports diet when you are traveling is to bring some foods with you. For example, you might want to bring items for before, during, and after the marathon:

Pre-marathon:
Bagels
Bananas
Peanut butter
Energy bars
Instant oatmeal
Raisins
Coffee or tea bags

During the marathon:
Gu
Clif Bloks
Sports beans
PowerBar Bites
Hard candy
Twizzlers
Peppermint patties
Tootsie rolls

Post marathon:
Gingerale or Cola (in case you feel sick)
V-8 juice (for salt)
Fruit yogurt or Go-gurt (protein-carb combo)
Cup-of-soup (fluid, salt, carbs)
Salted nuts (protein, salt)
Chocolate chip cookies (treat!)

Some runners choose a hotel with a microwave oven in the bedroom; others travel with an electric tea kettle for hot water (coffee, instant oatmeal, cup-of-soup). For example, elite marathoner Gelindo Bordin of Italy (known as a food-lover extraordinaire) schlepped not only his own pasta and grateable hard cheese to New York for the marathon, but also a small hot plate on which to cook in his hotel.

The 1992 New York City Marathon winner Willie Mtolo of South Africa also brought a hot plate to cook his traditional pre-marathon food: phutu, a cornmeal-based porridge. His cooking, however, promptly set off the hotel's fire detectors. Mtolo and his fiancée used towels to fan the cooking smells out the windows, waited for the firefighters to leave, then finished their meal in peace. Such can be the price of eating your familiar foods in preparation for the marathon!

- Request thick-crust pizza (with veggie toppings) rather than thin-crust pizza with pepperoni or sausage. If needed, blot off excess grease so you can carbo-load, not fat-load.
- At a salad bar, generously pile on the chickpeas, three-bean salad, beets, and fat-free croutons. Take plenty of bread. But don't fat-load on large amounts of butter, salad dressings, and mayonnaise-smothered pasta and potato salads.
- Baked potatoes are a super choice if you request them plain rather than drenched with butter, sour cream, and cheese toppings. For moistness, try mashing the potato with milk (special request) rather than gobs of butter. Some runners enjoy them with ketchup.
- Hearty soups (such as split pea, minestrone, lentil, vegetable, or noodle) accompanied by crackers, bread, a plain bagel, or an English muffin provide a satisfying, carbohydrate-rich meal.
- Both juices and soft drinks are rich in carbohydrates. Juices, however, are nutritionally preferable for vitamin C, potassium, and wholesome goodness.

Dinner:
- If possible, check out the restaurant beforehand to make sure that it offers wholesome carbohydrates (pasta, baked potatoes, rice, steamed vegetables, salad bars, homemade breads, fruit, juice), broiled foods, and lowfat options. To be on the safe side, save the exotic restaurants for after the marathon! Inquire how dishes are made and select the lower-fat options.
- Eat the breads and rolls either plain or with just a little butter. Replace butter-calories with more carbs: another slice of bread, a second potato, soup and crackers, juice, sherbet, or frozen yogurt.

Temptations for Travelers

Traveling marathoners can easily fat-load instead of carbo-load. Wisely choose your pre-marthon snacks and meals!

Temptation	Calories	% calories from fat	grams fat
Cinnabon	880	37%	36
Big Mac	540	48%	29
Pizza Hut Personal Pan Pizza, Pepperoni	610	43%	26
Au Bon Pain Chicken Caesar Asiago Wrap	610	41%	28
Mrs. Field's Chocolate Chip Cookie	210	43%	10
Cheesecake Factory, 1 slice Original	710	62%	49

- When ordering salads, always request the dressing be served on the side and use just a little bit. Otherwise, you may get as many as 400 calories of oil or mayonnaise—fatty foods that fill your stomach but leave your muscles unfueled.

Snacks and munchies:
- Pack your own snacks. Some suggestions include: whole-grain bagels, muffins, rolls, crackers, pretzels, fig bars, energy bars, granola bars, oatmeal-raisin cookies, graham crackers, hummus with pita bread, oranges, raisins, dried or fresh fruit, and juice boxes.
- Buy wholesome snacks at a convenience store: small packets of trail mix, bananas, dried fruit, yogurt, V-8 juice or fruit juice, bagel, hot pretzel, slice of thick-crust pizza, small sandwich, or cup of soup.

Summary

Traveling is fun but filled with food temptations. Do your best to stick to tried-and-true foods that you know will settle well and not upset your digestive system. Save the food experiments for after the marathon.

If you have any doubts about the availability of familiar foods, plan ahead and bring some "safe" foods with you—including the gels, energy bars, candies, and other sports foods you will want to consume during the marathon itself.

Breakfast for Travelers

If you're heading for a race out of town, this breakfast is portable, easy, and substantial. You can mix and match your own combinations of fruits and cereals.

In a plastic container with a lid, combine:

1/2 cup (40 g)	raw rolled oats
1/2 cup (30 g)	Grape-Nuts cereal or other cereal
1/4 cup (35 g)	raisins or other dried fruit
1/2 cup (35 g)	dry non-fat milk powder

When you are ready to eat, simply add 1 cup (240 ml) of cold water and shake!

YIELD: 1 serving
Calories per serving: 700

Carbohydrates:	135 g
Protein:	35 g
Fat:	3 g

Section IV
Weight and Marathoners

Chapter 14

Creating a
Calorie Budget

Many marathoners are on the "see food diet"; they see food and they eat it. They can naturally regulate a proper calorie intake and have little need to calculate calories. They simply eat when they are hungry and stop when they are content. But other marathoners see food and try to not eat it. They deem food as "fattening" and counter to their desires to be leaner, lighter runners. They have lost touch with their body's natural ability to regulate an appropriate food intake. They often do not eat when they are hungry (such as happens with severe reducing diets or skipping meals) and then overeat later in the day.

As a marathoner, you should eat your calories evenly throughout the day, not in a crescendo. That is, don't skimp on daytime meals only to spend your whole calorie budget in the evening! The better bet is to budget your calories so you eat enough at breakfast and lunch to support both an active life and a serious training program. Eating (wholesome) calories evenly throughout the day invests in high energy, added stamina, strength, and smooth running, to say nothing of better health.

If you struggle with energy lags, you might wonder how many calories are OK to eat to boost energy yet not "get fat." Knowing your calorie budget can help you estimate how much food is appropriate to:

- eat at each meal so you can avoid energy lags
- fuel-up and refuel from workouts
- lose desired weight and maintain energy for running
- feel energetic, train better, and feel good about your eating.

A calorie-counting approach to eating can help you eat the right amount of food at the right times. For example, if you skip breakfast and lunch (i.e., eat zero calories, zero fuel), you can clearly see why you lack energy for your afternoon training session. If you are weight-conscious, calorie information allows you to determine how much food you can eat for fuel yet still lose body fat.

Calculating Your Calorie Needs

If you struggle with eating intuitively and want to try working with a calorie budget, here is an easy formula to help you *estimate* your calorie needs. For more personalized advice, I highly recommend you consult with a registered dietitian who specializes in sports nutrition. Visit the American Dietetic Association's referral networks at www.eatright.org and www.SCANdpg.org to find a local sports dietitian.

1. To estimate your resting metabolic rate (RMR), that is, the amount of calories you need to simply breathe, pump blood, and be alive:

Multiply your weight (or a good weight for your body) by 10 calories per pound (or 22 calories per kilogram).
_____weight (lbs) x 10 calories/lb = _____ calories for your RMR

Example: if you weigh 120 pounds, you need approximately 1,200 calories (120 x 10) to simply do nothing all day except exist. If you are significantly overweight, use an adjusted weight: the weight that is halfway between your desired weight and your current weight.

2. Add more calories for daily activity—apart from your running and other purposeful exercise.
- 50% x RMR if you are moderately active throughout the day
- ~ 30-40% % if you are sedentary
- ~ 60-70% if you are very active (apart from your running or walking)

50% x _____RMR = _____ calories for daily activity

Example: a moderately active 120-pound woman who requires 1,200 calories for her resting metabolic rate needs about 600 more calories for activities of daily living. This totals 1,800 calories per day—without running.

3. Add more calories for your purposeful exercise. The general rule of thumb is 100 calories per mile, but more precisely, this depends upon your weight.

Body Weight lbs (kg)	Calories per mile
120 (55)	95
140 (64)	110
160 (73)	125
180 (82)	140

____exercise calories + _____daily activity + _____RMR = _____total calories

Example: a 120-pound woman who runs five miles per day burns about 475 calories while running. This brings her to about 2,275 calories per day to maintain her weight (475 running + 600 moderate daily activity + 1,200 RMR = 2.275). For simplicity, let's just say 2,300 calories.

Note: After a very hard workout or long run, marathoners tend to rest, recover and burn fewer calories than usual during the rest of their day. Observe if this happens with you. That is, do you tend to sit more than usual—reading more or watching more TV—after having done a long weekend run? If so, adjust your calorie needs accordingly!

4. To lose weight, target 80 to 90 percent of total calorie needs.

80% x _____total calories = _____ calories to reduce weight

Example: .80 x 2,300 calories = 1,840 calories, or more simply 1,800 calories/day
.90 x 2,300 calories = 2,070 calories, or more simply 2,100 calories/day
(Refer to chapter 15 for more guidance on weight loss.)

5. Now, take your calorie budget and divide it into three or four parts of the day. For the 120-pound woman on a diet, this comes to:

	Calories			Calories
Breakfast/snack	600-700	OR	Breakfast	500
Lunch/snack	600-700		Lunch	500-600
Dinner/snack	600-700		Lunch #2	300-400
			Dinner	500-600

The next step is to read food labels and get calorie information from websites (www.fitday.com, www.calorieking.com) to become familiar with the calorie content of the foods you commonly eat and then fuel your body according to the rules for a well-balanced diet.

Honor Hunger

I commonly hear marathoners complain, "Ever since I started training longer distances, I've been hungry all the time." They often feel confused by hunger and sometimes even feel guilty they are always eager to eat. One walker perceived her hunger as being bad and wrong.

Hunger is normal; it is essential for survival. Without hunger, we would waste away. Hunger is simply your body's way of requesting fuel. Hunger signals include needless fatigue, inability to focus and concentrate on the task at hand, moodiness, and cold hands and feet. These signals happen prior to a growling stomach, at which point you are too hungry.

The more you exercise, the hungrier you will get and the more fuel you will need. Plan to fuel up or refuel at least every four hours. You should not spend your day feeling hungry—even if you are on a reducing diet. (see chapter 15). If your 8:00 a.m. breakfast finds you hungry earlier than noon, your breakfast simply contained too few calories. You need a supplemental midmorning snack or a bigger breakfast that supplies about one-third of your day's calories.

Calorie Needs of Marathoners

Here are approximate calorie needs for marathoners of different weights who remain moderately active throughout the day. Take note: After a 10-miler, you may be ready to nap the rest of the day, and that would reduce your calorie needs! Be sure to adjust your calories according to your 24-hour energy expenditure.

Weight lbs (kg)	Approximate calorie needs for: daily living	5 mile-run or walk	10-mile run or walk
120 (55)	1,800	2,300	2,700
140 (64)	2,100	2,650	3,200
160 (73)	2,400	3,000	3,650
180 (82)	2,700	3,400	4,100

Come noontime, instead of thinking something is wrong with you because you are hungry again, enjoy lunch as being the second-most-important meal of the day. Morning runners, in particular, need a hearty lunch to refuel their muscles; afternoon runners need a respectable lunch and afternoon snack/second lunch to fuel their after-work training.

Whereas some runners like to satisfy their appetites with big meals, others prefer to divide their calories into mini-meals eaten every two hours. Eat however suits your training schedule and lifestyle. But whatever you do, eat when you are physically hungry. Hunger is simply your body's request for fuel. (The next chapter offers strategies for managing food that is mis-used as a "drug" to calm and reward yourself; keep reading!)

Summary

Just as you know how much money you can spend when you shop, some marathoners find it helpful to know how many calories they can enjoy spending when they eat. Weight-conscious marathoners, in particular, tend to undereat during the day and overeat at night. By targeting an appropriate (and often larger than normal) breakfast and lunch, you can fuel yourself evenly throughout the day. Learn to listen to your huger cues and respond by eating appropriately sized meals and snacks. Calorie-counting can be a tool to get in touch with how much is OK to eat, but calorie-counting should become needless as you relearn how to eat intuitively.

Banana Frostie

Whenever you are confronted with a surplus of bananas that are getting too ripe, peel them, cut them into chunks, and freeze them. Then, they'll be ready and waiting to be whipped into this frosty treat that tastes sinfully good. You'll think you are eating ice cream, but you are actually sneaking extra milk and fruit into your food plan!

Enjoy this as a yummy protein-carb recovery beverage.

Banana, in frozen chunks
1 cup (240 ml) lowfat milk

Optional: honey, brown sugar, or sugar substitute; dash of cinnamon, 1/4 teaspoon (1 ml) vanilla extract.
• Put the frozen banana chunks into a blender with milk.
• Blend on medium speed until smooth.
• Add sweetener and flavorings, as desired

Yield: 1 serving
Total calories: 230

Carbohydrates: 40 grams, Protein: 8 grams, Fat: 4 grams

Chapter 15

Weight Reduction
for Marathoners

Many overweight people commit to walking or running a marathon with hopes of accomplishing two goals:

1. getting fit and healthy
2. losing undesired body fat.

> I have been walking marathons for two years. Like the majority of walkers, I was hoping to lose weight, but that has not been the case for me. Many of my walking friends have even gained weight. Exercise alone does not suffice!

Becky Goodrum,
Cleveland, OH

> I suggest that people spend a year trying all the different diets they can find. Then, after having no success at achieving their goals, they gradually modify their normal eating habits. There are no quick fixes for weight loss. Period. Show me a quick fix, and I will show you how you are hurting your body.

John Correia,
San Diego, CA

Much to their dismay, they get fit, but some remain fatter than desired. As coach Lloyd Burnett of Mission, TX said, "I once trained three new marathoners who each lost 20 pounds in less than 6 months. Each of them made the commitment to be conscious about their calories and overall food intake. My training partner and I, on the other hand, have run almost 20 marathons but we each still weigh 220 pounds. I love my beer and he loves his tortillas. We're not willing to commit to the diet part of the event, even though we see the results all around us.

How to Lose Weight and Have Energy to Exercise

I spend hours counseling marathoners who struggle to lose weight. Most feel frustrated they just can't seem to shed those final few pounds. Inevitably, the first words they say to me are, "I know what I *should* do to lose weight. I just don't do it." They think they should follow a strict diet with rigid rules and regulations.

Wrong. Diets don't work. If diets did work, every marathoner who has ever been on a diet would be as thin as desired. The key to losing weight is to:

- stop attempting to *diet*
- start *eating healthfully.*

If you are dieting by day, only to "blow your diet" and overeat at night, think again.

How Much Is OK to Eat?

As I outlined in the chapter 14, active people need more than just a few calories to fuel themselves. To determine just how much you can appropriately eat, refer back to page 122. Note that your body requires an amazing amount of energy to pump blood, breathe, produce urine, grow hair, and simply exist. (Also note that your body requires those maintenance calories even if you are injured and unable to run.)

Weight Expectations

Although only nature knows the best weight for your body, the following guidelines offer a very general method to estimate a healthy weight. For a weight range, add or subtract 10 percent, according to your body frame and musculature. (These guidelines do not work for very muscular athletes.)

Women: 100 pounds (45 kg) for the first 5 feet (1.52 m) of height;
5 pounds (2.3 kg) per inch (2.5 cm) thereafter

Example: *A woman who is 5' 6" could appropriately weigh 130 lbs, or 117 lbs at the lower end if she is petite or 143 lbs if she is muscular. (1.7 m; 59 kg, 53-65 kg)*

Men: 106 pounds (48 kg) for the first 5 feet (1.52 m) of height;
6 pounds (2.7 kg) per inch (2.5 cm) thereafter

Example: *A man who is 5' 10" could appropriately weigh 166 lbs, or 150 lbs at the lower end if he is petite or 182 lbs if he is muscular. (1.8 m; 75.5 kg, 68-83 kg)*

Although marathoners commonly want to be lighter than the average person, heed this message: If you are striving to weigh significantly less than the weight estimated by this general guideline, think again. Pay attention to the genetic design for your body and don't struggle to get too light. The best weight goal is to be *fit* and *healthy* rather than sleek and skinny. Even heavy marathoners can be fit and healthy!

An appropriate reducing diet knocks off only *20 percent or less of your calorie needs*. Many weight-conscious marathoners try to eat as little as possible. That's a big mistake. Perhaps the following case study will help you understand why.

Ann, a 120-pound (54.5 kg) nurse, walks 5 miles most days. She requires about 2,200 to 2,300 calories to maintain her weight:

- 1,200 calories for her resting metabolic rate (10 calories per pound x 120 pounds)
- 600 calories for general daily activity (50% x 1,200 calories)
- 475 calories for her walk (95 calories per mile x 5 miles)

To appropriately lose weight, I recommended she cut her total calorie intake by 20 percent (about 400 to 500 calories), leaving her with 1,800 calories for her reducing plan.

To Ann, 1,800 sounded like too many calories. She exclaimed "I could never eat that much without turning into a blimp. If I can't lose weight on a 1,000-calorie diet, how could I possibly do so eating 1,800 calories? My metabolism is so *slow*. I seem to gain weight just smelling cookies."

Although Ann challenged my calorie recommendations, I suggested that she keep an open mind. The research on athletes' calorie needs suggests very few athletes

> I frequently see people gain weight during marathon training. They believe the training gives them license to eat anything and everything. Unfortunately, a 300-calorie dessert still shows up on the butt.
>
> *John Correia,*
> *San Diego CA*

actually do have slow metabolisms. Researchers have even studied active people like Ann who claim to maintain weight despite eating next to nothing. When carefully monitored, these women require the calories one would expect based on standard calculations. Their metabolisms were fine, but they had problems acknowledging how much food they actually ate—or how inactive they were in the non-training part of their day. Their nibbles on grapes, apples, rice cakes, and broken cookies added up! (For more information, refer to *Slow Metabolism Woes* in chapter 16.)

Because Ann claimed she ate far less than her peers, I suggested she heighten her awareness of her food intake by keeping food records. Food records can be extremely useful to help you understand your eating habits. For example, by listing *everything* that you eat, you might notice that you:

- eat when reading and don't even notice the portion
- eat too little at breakfast and lunch, only to overindulge at night
- diet Monday through Thursday, then splurge on weekends

Accurate food records can help you lose weight because people who keep food records tend to eat about 20 percent less—and that is an appropriate reducing diet

Five Keys to Successful Weight Reduction

Using your calorie guidelines, you can lose weight with the following five keys to successful weight reduction.

Key #1. *Eat just a little bit less. Don't get too hungry or you'll blow your diet.* For example, Lori, a receptionist and a runner, tried to self-impose the following bare bones diet:

Breakfast:	coffee	0 calories
Lunch:	dry salad	100
Snack:	large apple	150
Dinner:	frozen low-calorie meal	300
Total calories:		**550 (until she "blew it")**

This totaled *less than a quarter* of the 2,400 calories she required. No wonder she lacked energy for running. She'd often skip workouts and then at night eat everything in sight, only to get up the next morning with a food hangover. She'd then vow to get back on her diet, skip breakfast, skimp on lunch, lack energy to enjoy running, and blow her diet again at night. Her diet was too strict and unsustainable.

If you, like Lori, are trying to lose weight by eating as little as possible and exercising as hard as you can, remember that the less you eat, the more likely you are to blow your diet. Even if you can successfully restrict your intake, the less you eat, the more your body adjusts to having fewer calories. You will start to hibernate similar to what a bear does in winter when food is scarce. That is, your metabolic rate will drop to conserve calories and you'll feel lethargic, cold, and lack energy to exercise.

Research comparing dieters who either crash-dieted or followed a more reasonable reducing plan showed that both groups lost the same amount of body fat. The strict diet, however, caused the metabolic rate to drop. Why bother to eat next to nothing when you can lose weight with eating just 20 percent less than you need to maintain your weight?

Most of my female clients who want to lose body fat eat about 1,800 to 2,200 calories a day; male marathoners lose weight on about 2,200 to 2,600 calories. This is far more than most self-imposed 800- to 1,200-calorie diets. You need a substantial amount of energy to fuel your muscles and have energy to enjoy your training.

> " For a while I was trying to eat less so that I could weigh less, but I'd end up eating more and weighing more. I finally learned that if I eat sensible meals my weight is fine. I feel better and run better.
>
> *Candace Strobach, Kinnelon, NJ*
>
>

Key #2. *Be sure to eat adequately during the day, so that you'll be able to eat less (diet) at night.* For an appropriate reducing program, I recommend that you divide your calories evenly throughout the day. Because athletes tend to get hungry at least every four hours, an appropriate reduction diet for a 120-pound female marathoner might be:

Breakfast:	8 a.m.	500 calories
Lunch:	Noon	500
Lunch #2/Snack:	4 p.m.	400
Run:	6 p.m.	
Dinner:	8 p.m.	400

Your goal is to eat on a schedule to prevent yourself from getting too hungry. I call this my "eat more, lose weight" food plan.

Your training program may require creative meal scheduling if you exercise during meal times. For example, if you exercise at 6 p.m.—potentially at the height of your hunger—you might better enjoy your training if you eat part of your dinner beforehand. For example, trade in your 200-calorie dinner potato for a 200-calorie bagel at 5:00 p.m. Similarly, if you exercise at 6:00 a.m., you might enjoy greater energy if you eat part of your breakfast beforehand, such as a slice of toast and a glass of juice, and then eat the rest afterwards to recover from the workout and satisfy your hunger. (As I mentioned in chapter 8, you need to experiment with pre-exercise food to determine the right amount of calories that boosts your energy without making you feel heavy and sluggish.)

Successful Weight Loss

If blown diets are your downfall, I recommend you take the following steps:

- Eat a bigger breakfast and lunch—and observe the benefits (more energy, less hunger during the day and after dinner, better workouts)
- Enjoy a substantial afternoon snack or second lunch that ruins your evening appetite.
- "Diet" at night by eating smaller portions than usual.

Alternatively, a group of overweight men found success with this simple approach:

- Choose smaller portions at meals and snacks
- Cut back on sugary soft drinks
- Eat fewer high fat snack foods
- Consume less alcohol.

Some marathoners believe that exercising "on empty"— for example, running first thing in the morning before breakfast—helps them to burn more fat. While this may be true, keep in mind that *burning* fat does not equate to losing body fat. To lose body fat, you need to have created a calorie *deficit* for the whole day (not just during workouts). People who exercise on empty lack the fuel they need to sustain long, strong workouts. Hence, they burn fewer calories than someone who is properly fueled before exercise. They also experience extreme hunger later on and often get derailed by the Cookie Monster.

Key #3. *Eat an appropriate amount of fat.* If you are currently eating a high-fat diet filled with butter, mayonnaise, salad dressing, French fries, and pepperoni, you should cut back on these and other fatty foods. Excess dietary fat easily turns into excess body fat, if not clogged arteries.

On the other hand, if you are trying to knock all the fat out of your diet—thinking that if you eat fat, you'll instantly get fat—think again and see chapter 7. Fat can be helpful for dieters because it takes longer to digest and provides a nice feeling of satisfaction that can prevent you from scrounging around the kitchen, looking for something tasty to eat. Runners who try to eat a no fat diet commonly live with a nagging hunger, to say nothing of feelings of denial and deprivation.

One study reported that dieters who were instructed to eat 1,200 calories of a high fat diet actually lost more body fat than the group who

Why Are You Eating?

Food has many roles. It satisfies hunger, fuels muscles, is a pleasurable part of social gatherings and celebrations, rewards us at the end of a stressful day, and has a calming effect. If you tend to eat for reasons other than fuel, think HALT and ask yourself, why do I want to eat? Is it because I am:

Hungry?

Angry or Anxious?

Lonely?

Tired?

If you are eating inappropriately, remember that no amount of food will solve any problem. Don't start eating if you know you'll have problems stopping.

were instructed to eat 1,200 calories of a very-lowfat diet. Why? Because the high-fat dieters were better able to comply with their regimen. You, too, may enjoy better success with fat loss if you give yourself reasonable calorie and fat budgets to spend on the foods that you truly enjoy eating. There is a diet portion of any food—including French fries and cookies! (Refer to Chapter 7 for more information on what a 25-percent fat diet looks like.)

Key #4. *Try to lose weight when life is smooth.* You don't have to lose weight every day. Losing weight requires significant mental energy to keep reminding yourself, "I'd rather be leaner than eat more calories." Some days you may lack that mental energy. For example, Paul, a lawyer and runner who wanted to lose five pounds before the Chicago Marathon, was stressed out by his demanding workload, training schedule, and family problems. Although he wanted to drop a few pounds, he lacked the mental energy he needed to cut calories. At the end of the day, he'd inevitably succumb to ice cream, his reward for having survived the day.

I reminded Paul that he is only human, with a limited amount of mental and physical energy. Rather than punish himself for lacking energy to restrict calories, he needed to accept the fact that he was stressed and in need of comfort. Like it or not, food provided that comfort.

> " Do not be obsessed with the numbers on the scale. With time and training, you will learn at what weight you can perform well. Listening to your body is more accurate than any scale. "
>
> *Mike Czech,*
> *Edison, NJ*

I recommended that Paul let go of his current goal to *lose* fat and focus instead on *maintaining* his weight and fueling his muscles appropriately. Well-fueled muscles could enhance his running more than dropping a few pounds. I also reminded Paul he had the rest of his life to lose excess body fat. In this already stressful season in his life, he might be happier removing the additional self-imposed stress of trying to lose weight. He reluctantly agreed with that reality.

Stressful times are often poor times to try to reduce body fat. Rather, focus on exercising regularly to help cope with stress and on eating healthful foods every four hours to keep your appetite under control. Marathoners who are both stressed and hungry can too easily succumb to overeating. Yet, no amount of food will solve any problem. In fact, it only adds to your feeling out of control.

Key #5. *Have realistic weight goals.* Weight is more than a matter of willpower; genetics plays a large role. If you are exercising regularly, fueling appropriately during the day, eating lighter at night, and waking up hankering for breakfast but still have not lost weight, perhaps you have an unrealistic goal? Perhaps you have no excess fat to lose and are already lean for your genetic blueprint? Like it or not, weight is more than a matter of willpower. Although you might wish for a sleeker physique, nature might want you to be more substantial.

> **Planned weight loss— one to two pounds per week—and marathon training don't mix. The weight loss should occur prior to or during the early stages of the training program. Once mileage and quality of training increase, the nutrition focus should be on replenishment, not deficit, of calories.**
>
> *Ronnie Carda,*
> *Madison, WI*

Marsha, the novice marathoner, was short and had thin hair and big thighs, "just like my mother and sisters." Although she put no effort into trying to grow taller or thicken her hair, she obsessed about the fat on her thighs and spent lots of energy trying to reduce them.

I reminded Marsha that although she could remodel her body to a certain extent, she couldn't totally redesign it. Plain and simple, walkers and runners, like fruits and dogs, come in varying sizes and shapes. No one body type is right or wrong.

In order to determine an appropriate weight for your body, I recommend you stop looking at the scale and start looking at your family. Imagine yourself at a family reunion.

- How do you compare to other members of your family?
- Are you currently leaner than they are? fatter? the same?
- If leaner, are you struggling to stay that way?

If you are significantly leaner, you may already be underfat for your body.

I counsel many runners who put their lives on hold, struggling to lose a final few pounds. As Marsha said as she grabbed onto her thighs, "I hate being seen in running shorts. But no matter how much I exercise, I can't get rid of these fat thighs. I must be doing something wrong."

Marsha was simply trying to get to a weight that was abnormal for her genetics. She was already leaner that other members of her family. I helped her to understand the reason why women (as compared to men) have "fat thighs": the fat in the thigh area is sex-specific. It is a storehouse of energy for potential pregnancy and breast-feeding and is supposed to be there. Just as women have breast tissue, women also have thigh tissue. Women have fatter thighs than men because women are women. Marsha needed to accept the realities of being a woman and stop comparing herself to the magazine models who indeed have rare physiques.

If you are wasting your time and energy complaining about your body, keep this is perspective: Life is a gift, too short to be spent obsessing about food and weight. Be appreciative of all our body can do for you—such as endure marathon training—and stop criticizing your body for what it is not. You can be fit, healthy and happy at any size. You can also be miserable at your "perfect weight" if the cost of attaining that weight is yo-yo dieting, poor nutrition, lack of energy to exercise, guilt for eating, a sense of failure that crushes your self-esteem, and, of course, poor marathon performance.

Summary

Food is fuel. You need to fuel your muscles appropriately even if you are trying to lose weight. Be realistic about your expectations and remember:

- the thinnest marathoner may not be the fastest marathoner.
- the best-fueled marathoners will always win with good nutrition.

Also remember the following keys to successful weight control:
1. Deduct only 20 percent (or less) of your calorie budget; don't starve yourself.
2. Fuel during the day, then diet at night. Being hungry when you wake up can be a sign you lost weight overnight.
3. Include a little bit of (healthful) fat at each meal to keep you from feeling hungry during the day and also from feeling denied.
4. Strive to maintain weight on stress-filled days and lose weight on gentler days.
5. Honor your genetics and be realistic with your weight goals.

Chicken Noodle Soup

If you are hoping to shed a few pounds, chicken noodle soup is an excellent choice for supper. Steaming hot, you need to eat it slowly—a good tactic for curbing calorie intake. Soup is also an easy-to-digest pre-game and/or recovery meal that offers fluids, sodium, carbohydrates, and protein. After a cold-weather run, what could be nicer than coming home to a nice bowl of homemade soup!

2 chicken breasts, with bone
3 cups (24 ounces; 720 ml) chicken broth, from bouillon cubes or canned
2 carrots, diced
2 stalks celery, diced
1 small onion, diced
2 cups (330 g) corn, frozen or canned
Salt and pepper to taste
8 ounces (240 g) pasta, uncooked (e.g. small shells, bow ties, etc.)

1. Drop two chicken breasts (bone in) into a big pot.
2. Add enough broth just to cover the chicken, about 3 cups.
3. Cover, cook until chicken is done, about 20 to 30 minutes.
4. Remove chicken, let it cool for about 10 minutes, cut or pull it off the bone, and then put the chicken back in the broth.
5. While the chicken is cooling, skim the fat off the broth.
6. Cut up the carrots, celery and onion. Add them to the broth with the chicken.
7. Cook for another 30 to 60 minutes; then add the corn.
8. While the corn is cooking, in a separate pot, cook the pasta (shape of your choice).
9. Add the cooked pasta to the soup; add more chicken broth, salt and pepper, as desired.

Yield: 5 servings (as a part of a meal)
Total Calories: 1,500
Calories per serving: 300

Carbohydrate: 50 g, Protein: 20 g Fat: 2 g

Recipe courtesy of Christie Welsh. Reprinted with permission from *Food Guide for Soccer: Tips and Recipes from the Pros* by Gloria Averbuch and Nancy Clark MS RD. Meyer & Meyer Sport 2010.

Chapter 16

Dieting Gone Awry

Fueled by the "thinner is better" philosophy, some marathoners consider food to be a fattening enemy rather than a friendly fuel. They fear that eating satisfying meals will make them fatter and slower. Some weight-conscious marathoners deny themselves adequate nutrition until they get to the "perfect weight" (an elusive goal).

Marathoners who strive to be "perfectly" thin commonly pay a high price: poor nutrition, poorly fueled muscles, stress fractures, nagging injuries, loss of menses (in women), to say nothing of reduced stamina, endurance, and performance. In their overconcern about their bodies, dieting marathoners forget this formula:

appropriate eating + regular exercise = appropriate weight

Whereas Chapter 15 offered guidance about how to lose weight and maintain energy for walking or running, this chapter provides an additional perspective to help resolve the obsessions with food and weight that happen when dieting goes awry. These obsessions are most common in active women. Hence this chapter focuses mostly on women, but if you are a man who struggles with food, the information can help you, as well.

Women and Weight

Why is weight such a big issue among women? Let's look at the possible explanations.

1. Women naturally have more body fat than men, and many women deem this as undesirable. Never the less, women need more body fat to:
- protect their ability to create and nourish healthy babies
- provide a storehouse of calories for pregnancy and breast feeding

This essential body fat is stored not only in the breasts but also in the hips, abdomen, and upper legs. That's why women tend to have heavier thighs than most men.

Whereas 11 to 13 percent of a woman's body weight is essential fat stores, only 3 to 5 percent of a man's body weight is essential body fat. Hence, women who try to achieve the "cut look" of male athletes commonly end up having to starve themselves, then they binge and obsess about food as they struggle to reach an unnatural image.

Surveys of top women athletes suggest even the very lean, front-of-the-pack women runners wish they could be lighter. No wonder dieting and disordered eating patterns prevail!

2. Women tend to have distorted body images. The Madison Avenue image that adorns every storefront and magazine ad leads us to believe that nature makes all women universally lean. Any aberration is thought to be a result of gluttony and lack of willpower. Wrong!

Nature makes us in different sizes and shapes, like it or not. If all the marathoners who are discontent with their weight could only learn to accept and love their bodies as being "good enough," eating disorders would be rare. Case in point, a food-obsessed 5'7" and 115 pounds marathoner who lamented, "I don't have the gaunt look of the really fast runners. I really wish I could weigh 110." She was unable to see that she was already very lean; a normal, healthy weight for a 5'7" woman is 135 pounds! She was training harder and harder to burn calories and lose body fat, not to enhance performance.

The Slow Metabolism Woes

Some marathoners comment the fitter they are, the fewer calories they need. They perceive themselves as being energy-efficient; they commonly complain about being cold all the time, feeling lethargic, and (among women) lacking regular menstrual cycles. As elite runner Priscilla Welch once said, "I'm amazed at what nonrunners can tuck away." Perhaps you've heard your buddies express similar complaints:

- I eat less than my friends but I still don't lose weight. There must be something wrong with my metabolism.
- I maintain weight on only 1,000 calories per day. I want to lose a few pounds, but I can't imagine eating any less.
- I run at least eight miles every day and eat only one meal a day. I can't understand why I don't lose weight.

These comments raise questions about metabolic efficiency. Does nature slow an athlete's athlete's metabolism to protect him or her from getting too thin?

According to Dr. Jack Wilmore, exercise physiologist at the University of Texas at Austin, the energy-efficient athlete does not exist. His research suggests that metabolic rate is closely tied to muscle mass. Many of the marathoners who restrict calories end up burning muscle tissue for energy. Hence, they tend to have less muscle mass. Consequently, they require fewer calories. "Plain and simple, athletes who have well-developed muscles require more calories than those who have less muscle."

Often overlooked is how few calories a marathoner burns when he or she is not exercising. After a long run, marathoners can easily take a nap, read the paper, or relax. In the 24-hour day, they may be less active than before they started marathon training—when they would have mowed the lawn, played actively with their children, and been more active throughout the entire day. Hence, the trick to increasing calorie needs may be to remain active throughout the entire day, not just when training.

Women, Running, and Amenorrhea

If you are a marathoner who previously had regular menstrual periods but currently has stopped menstruating, you are experiencing amenorrhea. Although

> I'm saddened by how many women runners have eating disorders. I know, because I struggled with food for a while. I can pick out all the runners who are currently struggling. They think they have a secret but they don't. I can remember how tired I used to be. Then, I started eating better and my running got better. I was surprised by how well food worked. It really helps runners to run better!
>
> *Gordon Bakoulis, New York City*

you may think the loss of menses is because you are too thin or are exercising too much, thinness and exercise are generally not the causes of amenorrhea. After all, many very thin marathoners do have regular menses. Studies have shown that both regularly menstruating and amenorrheic athletes commonly have the same amount of body fat.

But the question remains unanswered: Why, given a group of women who have a similar training program and the same low percent of body fat, do some experience menstrual problems and others don't? Marathoners with amenorrhea often struggle to maintain an unhealthfully low weight. The cost of achieving this leanness is inadequate nutrition and, consequently, loss of menses.

Athletic amenorrhea is commonly a nutritional problem and sometimes a red flag for an eating disorder. If you stop having regular menstrual periods, be sure to consult with both your gynecologist and sports nutritionist for professional guidance.

Health Risks Associated with Amenorrhea

Although you may deem amenorrhea a desirable side effect of exercise because you no longer have to deal with the hassles and possible discomfort of monthly menstrual periods, amenorrhea can lead to undesirable problems that can interfere with your health and ability to perform at your best. These problems include:

- almost a three times higher incidence of stress fractures
- premature osteoporosis (weakening of the bones) that can affect your bone health in the not-too-distant future
- inability to conceive should you want to have a baby.
- future difficulty conceiving, even with resumption of menses.

If the amenorrhea is caused by very restrictive eating, it can be a symptom of pain and unhappiness in your life. Living in a smokescreen of hunger seems less painful than feeling other feelings.

Amenorrheic women who resume menses can restore some of the bone density lost during their months of amenorrhea, particularly if they are younger than seventeen years. But they do not restore all of it. Hence, your goal should be to minimize the damages of amenorrhea by eating appropriately and taking the proper steps to regain your menstrual periods. Remember: Food is fuel, healthful and health-giving, not a fattening enemy.

Resolving Amenorrhea

The possible changes required to resume menses include:

- training 5 to 15 percent less (50 minutes instead of an hour)
- consuming 10 percent more calories each week, until you ingest an appropriate amount given your activity level. For example, if you have been eating 1,000 calories a day, eat 100 more calories per day for a total of 1,100 total calories a day during the first week (or even for 2 to 3 days); eat a total of 1200 calories per day the second week; 1,300 the third week, and so on. (See Chapter 14 for how to determine an appropriate calorie intake.)

How to Boost Your Food Plan

If you maintain weight despite eating minimal calories and are spending way too much time thinking about food, here's a sample food plan to help you start to fuel your body better. Because you are adding essential (not excess) calories to get your body out of hibernation, you will be unlikely to "get fat."

Gradually add 100 calories every few days (or every week, if that feels safer) and observe the benefits: you will likely feel stronger, happier, warmer; sleep better; have bettter workouts, and think less about food.

Your best bet, to help you through this process of relearning how to eat appropriately, is to go to www.eatright.org or www.SCANdpg.org and use the referral networks to find a local sports dietitian who can provide personalized advice.

Baseline Menu: 1,000 calories		Improved 1,800-calorie Menu	
Breakfast:			
Special K, 1 cup (30 g)	100	Special K, 2 cups	200
Milk, 1/2 cup	50	Milk 1/2 cup	50
		Banana	100
Snack			
Apple, average	100	Apple	100
		Almonds, 14	100
Lunch			
Salad	100	Salad	100
Tuna, small can	100	Tuna, lg can	200
		Yogurt, 1 cup	100
		Crackers	100
Snack			
Energy bar	250	Energy bar	250
Dinner			
Chicken breast, 4 oz	200	Chicken breat	200
Broccoli, 2 cups	100	Brocoli, 2 cups	100
		Rice, 1/2 cup	100
		Milk, 1 cup	100
Total: 1,000 calories		**1,800**	

Some amenorrheic runners have resumed menses with just reduced exercise and no weight gain. For example, an injured runner who totally stops training might resume menses within two months. Others resume menstruating after rebuilding and restoring five pounds (or less) of health. And despite what you may think, this small amount of weight gain tends to include muscle-weight and does not result in your "getting fat."

If you have stopped menstruating and believe that poor eating may be part of the problem, you should consider getting a nutrition checkup with a registered dietitian who specializes in sports nutrition (see the sidebar below, Steps to Resolve Eating Disorders).

The following tips may help you resume menses or at least rule out nutrition-related factors.

1. *Throw away the bathroom scale.* Rather than striving to achieve a certain number on the scale, let your body weigh what it weighs. Focus on how healthy you feel and how well you perform, rather than on the number you weigh.

Steps to Resolve Eating Disorders

If you are spending too much time obsessing about food, weight and exercise, seek help and information by contacting:

National Eating Disorders Association (information and referral network) *www.NationalEatingDisorders.org*

American Dietetic Association (referral network) *www.eatright.org*

Something Fishy Website on Eating Disorders (information and referral network) *www.something-fishy.org*

Gurze Books (recommended self-help books) *www.bulimia.com*

If you suspect your training partner or friend is struggling with food issues, speak up! Anorexia and bulimia are self-destructive eating behaviors that may signal underlying depression and can be life-threatening. Here are some helpful tips:

- Approach the person gently but be persistent. Say that you are worried about her health. She, too, may be concerned about her loss of concentration, light-headedness, or chronic fatigue. These health changes are more likely to be a stepping stone to accepting help, since the person clings to food and exercise for feelings of control and stability.
- Don't discuss weight or eating habits. Address the fundamental problems of life. Focus on unhappiness as the reason for seeking help. Point out how anxious, tired, and/or irritable the person has been lately. Emphasize that she doesn't have to be that way.
- Post a list of resources (with tear-off websites at the bottom) where the person will see it (see resources listed above).

Remember that you are not responsible and can only try to help. Your power comes from using community resources and health professionals, such as a counselor, nutritionist, or eating disorders clinic.

2. *If you have weight to lose, don't crash-diet* but rather slightly cut back on your food intake by cutting out only 100 to 200 calories. Severe dieters commonly lose their menstrual periods, suggesting that amenorrhea is an adaptation to the calorie deficit produced either by low calorie intake alone or by increased energy expenditure via exercise. In particular, rapid weight loss may predispose you to amenorrhea. By following a healthy reducing program, such as outlined in Chapter 15, you'll not only have greater success with long-term weight loss, but also have enough energy to run.

3. *If you are at an appropriate weight, practice eating as you did as a child:* Eat when you are hungry, stop when you are content. Don't stop eating just because you think you should. If you are always hungry and are constantly obsessing about food, you are undoubtedly trying to eat too few calories. Chapter 14 can help you determine an appropriate calorie intake and eating schedule that may differ from your current routine, particularly if you yo-yo between starving and bingeing.

4. *Eat adequate protein.* Research has suggested that amenorrheic runners tend to eat less protein than their regularly menstruating counterparts. In one study, 82 percent of the amenorrheic women ate less than the recommended dietary allowance for protein. Vegetarians, in particular, need to be sure to consume adequate protein (see Chapter 6).

5. *Eat at least 20 percent of your calories from fat.* Amenorrheic marathoners commonly are afraid of eating fat. They think that if they eat fat, they'll get fat. Although excess calories from fat are easily fattening, some fat (20 to 30 percent of total calories) is an appropriate part of a healthy sports diet. For most active women, this translates into about 40 to 60 or more grams of fat per day. Clearly, this differs from a no-fat diet and allows lean meats, peanut butter, nuts, olive oil, and other wholesome foods and healthful fats that balance a sports diet (see Chapter 7).

6. *Maintain a calcium-rich diet.* You should choose a high-calcium diet to help maintain bone density. Because you build peak bone density in your teens and early adult years, your goal is to protect against future problems with osteoporosis by eating calcium-rich foods today. As I mentioned in Chapter 1, a safe target is at least 1,000 milligrams of calcium per day if you are between nineteen and fifty years old, and 1,200 to 1,300 milligrams of calcium per day if you are amenorrheic or post-menopausal. This is the equivalent to including a serving of milk, yogurt, and other dairy or calcium-rich foods at each meal in the day.

Chapter 1 provides guidelines for getting an optimal amount of calcium. Although you may cringe at the thought of spending so many calories on dairy foods, remember that milk is not an "optional fluid" but rather a wholesome food that contains many important nutrients. Some research also suggests women who consume three or more glasses of milk or yogurt per day tend to be leaner than those who do not consume as much dairy.

Calcium is only one factor that affects bone density. There is a genetic factor to osteoporosis; if your mother or grandmother has/had osteoporosis, you are more likely to get the disease. Other factors that contribute to your risk for osteoporosis include being too thin with too little muscle tugging on bones to keep them strong, doing inadequate muscle-building exercise, and having low levels of estrogen. Because you are athletic, your bones benefit from the protective effect of exercise, particularly strength training. But exercise does not override the health dangers of being too thin, consuming inadequate calcium or lacking estrogen (as occurs with amenorrhea).

Summary

Food should be one of life's pleasures, a fun part of your marathon-training program, and a protector of your good health. If you spend too much time thinking about food as being a fattening enemy, I highly recommend you consult with a registered dietitian who specializes in sports nutrition and eating disorders (use the referral network at www.eatright.org and www.SCANdpg.org). This professional can help you transform your food fears into healthful fueling, so your body can support your goals of training for and completing the marathon in good health, with high energy, and finding peace with food and your body.

Shrimp with Feta and Tomatoes

Shrimp is a low fat, low calorie source of protein—perfect for weight-conscious runners. Enjoy shrimp as a part of this quick and easy to prepare meal. Serve with rice and a salad.

1 tablespoon oil
2 to 4 cloves garlic, chopped (or 1/4 teaspoon garlic powder)
1 pound cleaned, deveined shrimp
1 28-ounce can crushed or diced tomatoes
4 ounces feta cheese, crumbled
Optional: 1/2 cup chopped fresh parsley; 1/2 teaspoon dried oregano
1. In a nonstick skillet, heat the oil and sauté the garlic and shrimp until the shrimp turns pink, about 1 minute.
2. Add the tomatoes (and oregano) and simmer for 2 to 5 minutes.
3. Add the crumbled feta. Add the parsley just before serving.

Yield: 4 servings, **Total calorie**s: 1,000, **One serving:** 250 calories

Carbohydrate: 9 g, Protein: 28 g, Fat: 11 g

With one cup of rice: 450 calories
Carbohydrate 53 g, Protein 30 g, Fat 13 g

Reprinted with permission from *Nancy Clark's Sports Nutrition Guidebook, Fourth Edition.* Human Kinetics, 2008.

How to Gain
Weight Healthfully

> When I started to train for the marathon, I was too busy to eat. I lost weight and felt self-conscious about my scrawny legs and skinny body. I contemplated quitting the training program, because I was afraid I'd turn into a bag of bones. Instead, I made an effort to better plan my sports diet. I started drinking lots more juice and milk, and having a peanut butter and honey sandwich before bed.

Justin Holmes,
Wellesley MA

If you are among the minority of marathoners who struggles with being too thin, food may seem a medicine, meals a burden, and food shopping a budget-breaker. Gaining weight is hard work! Through strength training and diet, you can change your physique to a certain extent, but first, be sure you have a realistic goal based on your genetic blueprint and the weights of other people in your genetic family.

- Was your mother or father very slim at your age?
- When did he or she gain weight?
- What does he or she look like now?

If, at your age, a parent was similarly thin, you probably are genetically predisposed to being thin and may have trouble adding pounds. Some people are simply "hard gainers." For example, in an overfeeding study on identical twins, some pairs of twins gained more weight than others, despite the fact that everyone overate by an equal amount—1,000 extra calories per day. In another study, some subjects who theoretically should have gained eleven pounds during a month-long overfeeding study gained an average of only six pounds. Why the difference? Perhaps the "hard gainers" fidgeted more than others; fidgeting can burn an extra 300 to 700 calories per day! In comparison, "easy gainers" tend to enjoy sitting calmly.

Six Rules for Gaining Weight

If you are a hard gainer, you can try to fidget less (unlikely!) and consume more calories than you expend. Adding muscle-building exercise such as weightlifting helps convert the extra calories into muscle rather than fat.

I encourage underweight marathoners to consume an additional 500 to 1,000 calories per day. If you are committed to the weight-gain process, you can expect to gain one-half to one pound per week, perhaps more depending on your age. For example, high school and collegiate athletes may bulk-up more easily than the fully mature 35-year-old who is genetically skinny.

The trick to successful weight gain is to pay careful attention to these six important rules.

1. *Eat consistently.* Have at least three or four hearty meals plus one or two additional snacks daily. Do not skip meals! You may not feel hungry for lunch if you've had a big breakfast, but you should eat regardless. Otherwise, you'll miss out on important calories that you need to accomplish your goal.

2. *Eat larger portions.* Some people think they need to buy expensive weight-gain powders. They don't need special supplements; standard food works fine. The only

reason commercial powders "work" is because they provide additional calories. For example, one marathoner religiously drank the recommended three glasses per day of a 300-calorie weight-gain shake. This gave him an extra 900 calories and the desired results. Although he credited the weight-gain formula for his success, he could have less expensively consumed those calories with supermarket foods. I suggested that he invest his food budget in readily available foods:

- a bigger bowl of cereal
- a larger piece of fruit
- an extra sandwich for lunch or a large sub sandwich
- three potatoes at dinner instead of two
- a taller glass of milk.

When he did this, he met his goal of 1,000 extra calories per day and continued to see the desired results.

3. *Select higher calorie foods, but not higher fat foods.* Excess fat calories easily convert into body fat that fattens you up rather than bulks up your muscles. The best bet for extra calories is to choose carbohydrate-dense foods that have more calories than an equally enjoyable counterpart (see sidebar, How to Boost Your Calories). These extra carbohydrates will give you the energy you need to do muscle-building exercise. By reading food labels, you'll be able to make the best choices.

How to Boost Your Calories

Choose more:	Calories	Amount	Instead of:	Calories	Amount
Cranberry juice	170	8 oz (240 ml)	Orange juice	110	8 ounces
Grape juice	160	8 oz (240 ml)	Grapefruit juice	100	8 ounces
Banana	170	1 large	Apple	130	1 large
Granola	780	1.5 cups (150 g)	Bran flakes	200	1.5 cups (60 g)
Grape-Nuts	660	1.5 cups (175)	Cheerios	160	1.5 cups (45 g)
Corn	140	1 cup (165 g)	Green beans	40	1 cup (120 g)
Carrots	45	1 cup (150 g)	Zucchini	30	1 cup (180 g)
Split pea soup	130	1 cup (240 ml)	Vegetable soup	80	1 cup
Baked beans	260	1 cup (260 g)	Rice	190	1 cup (160 g)

4. *Drink lots of juice and lowfat milk.* Beverages are a simple way to increase your calorie intake. Replace part or all of the water you drink with calorie-containing fluids. One high school athlete gained 13 pounds over the summer by simply subtracting water and adding six glasses of cranapple juice (about 1,000 calories) to his standard daily diet. Extra juices are not only a great source of calories and fluids but also of carbohydrates to keep your muscles well fueled.

5. *Do strength training (push-ups, weightlifting) to stimulate muscular development, so that you bulk up instead of fatten up.* Note that extra exercise, not extra protein, is the key to muscular development. One skinny marathoner expressed concern the long runs would result in weight loss rather than weight

gain. I reminded him that exercise tends to stimulate the appetite. Yes, a hard run may temporarily "kill" your appetite right after the workout because your body temperature is elevated, but within a few hours when you have cooled down, you will be plenty hungry. The more you exercise, the more you'll want to eat—assuming you make the time to do so.

6. *Be patient.* If you are in high school or college and don't easily bulk-up this year, you may do so more easily as you get older. Know that you can be a strong marathoner by being well fueled and well trained. Your skinny legs may hurt your self-esteem more than your athletic ability.

Apple Brown Betty

This is a yummy way to boost your intake of calories—as well as your of fruit and carbs. A wholesome dessert for a hungry marathoner.

11 sheets (1/3 box; 340 g) graham crackers
1/4 cup (60 g) soft margarine, melted
6 large (1.2 kg) apples, unpeeled
3/4 cup (145 g) brown sugar
1 teaspoon (4 g) cinnamon
1/2 cup (120 ml) water
Optional: 1/4 tsp. (1 g) nutmeg
1/4 tsp (1 g) cloves
2 tablespoons (30 ml) lemon juice
1/2 cup (70 g) raisins and/or chopped nuts

1. Crush the graham crackers into crumbs by placing them in a plastic bag and rolling them with a rolling pin or a bottle.
2. In a bowl, combine the crumbs with the melted margarine.
3. Put one-third of the mixture in the bottom of a 2-quart (2-liter) casserole dish.
4. Core and slice the apples into thin wedges and put them into a bowl. Sprinkle the apple wedges with sugar, cinnamon. and other spices and lemon juice, as desired.
5. Put the apple slices into the baking dish; add 1/2 cup water and then the rest of the graham cracker crumbs.
6. Cover and bake at 350°F (175°C) for 25 minutes; uncover, then bake another 15 minutes to crispen.

Total calories: 2,500
8 servings
Calories per serving: 310
Carbohydrate: 58 g, Protein: 1 g, Fat: 8 g

Summary

The key to gaining weight is to consistently consume more calories that you currently enjoy. Simple ways to do this include choosing calorie-dense foods, eating larger portions at meals (particularly breakfast and lunch, because dinners tend to be large enough), and replacing water with juices and lowfat milk. Strength training is an important part of a weight gain program, so you add more muscle than fat.

Afterword

Running 26.2 miles may seem unimaginable when you embark upon your first five-minute jog. But it can become a dream come true, as witnessed in the thousands of runners who participate in marathons year after year. Training wisely is an essential part of marathon preparation, and so is fueling wisely. With no gas in your tank, you won't get very far!

If you train wisely and fuel appropriately, you too will discover that marathoning is one of life's pleasures, a source of great pride—and also one of the easiest and most time-efficient ways to get into shape, manage your weight, and invest in future good health.

Wherever your running path takes you—5Ks, 10 milers, half-marathons or the full marathon—dedicate yourself to good nutrition. You'll always feel better, run better, and be a winner with a sports diet that fuels your muscles and nourishes your soul!

Eat wisely, be well, and enjoy miles of smiles.

With best regards,

Nancy

Additional Resources

To find a local sports nutritionist:

The American Dietetic Association offers two referral networks:
www.eatright.org
www.SCANdpg.org

Online book catalogs:

Nutrition books:Nutrition Counseling and Education Services
www.ncescatalog.com

Eating disorders books: Gurze Books
www.bulimia.com

Fitness and sports nutrition books: Human Kinetics
www.humankinetics.com

Recommended Reading

Benardot, Dan. *Advanced Sports Nutrition.* Human Kinetics, 2006.
Clark, Nancy. *Nancy Clark's Sports Nutrition Guidebook, Fourth Edition.* Human
    Kinetics, 2008.
Colberg, Sheri. *Diabetic Athlete's Handbook.* Human Kinetics, 2009
Duyff, Roberta. *The American Dietetic Association's Complete Food and Nutrition
    Guide.* Chronimed Publishing, 2006.
Freedman, Rita. B*odyLove: Learning to Like Our Looks and Ourselves.* Gurze
    Books, 2002
Heffner, M. *The Anorexia Workbook: How to accept yourself, heal your suffering
    & reclaim your life* 2004
Hirschmann, Jane and Carol Munter. *When Women Stop Hating Their Bodies:
    Freeing Yourself from Food and Weight Obsession.* Fawcett Books, 1997.
Larsen-Meyer, Enette. *Vegetarian Sports Nutrition.* Human Kinetics, 2007
LoBue, Andrea and Marsea Marcus. *The Don't Diet, Live-It! Workbook: Healing
    Food, Weight & Body Issues.* Gurze Books, 1999.
McCabe, Randi and Traci McFarlane. *The Overcoming Bulimia Workbook.* Gurze
    Books, 2003
Powers, P. and R. Thompson. *The Exercise Balance: What's Too Much, Too Litte,
    Just Right.* 2008
Satter, Ellyn. *Secrets of Feeding a Healthy Family.* Kelcy Press, 2008.
Satter, Elly. *Your Overweight Child: Helping Without Harming,* Kelcy Press   2005
Siegel, Michelle, Judith Brisman, and Margot Weinshel. *Surviving an Eating Disorder:
    Perspectives and Strategies for Families and Friends.* HarperCollins, 2009
Tribole, Evelyn and Elyse Resch. *Intuitive Eating: A revolutionary program that
    works* St. Martins Press, 2003

Textbooks for coaches and professionals:

Manore M, N Meyer & J Thompson. *Sport Nutrition for Health and Performance.* Human Kinetics 2009

Wiliams, M. *Nutrition for Health, Fitness & Sport*, McGraw-Hill, 2009

Internet Resources

Sports and sports nutrition:
Nancy Clark, MS, RD
www.nancyclarkrd.com
Links to nutrition articles and other nutrition sources; information on teaching materials

Australian Institute of Sport
www.ausport.gov.au/ais
Comprehensive information on physical fitness and nutrition

Gatorade Sports Science Institute
www.gssiweb.com

FitDay.com
www.FitDay.com
This site allows you to track and assess your food intake.

Health and nutrition:
International Food Information Council Foundation
http://www.foodinsight.org
This site features information on food safety and nutrition.

Medical information
www.WedMD.com
Offers both medical and nutrition information

U.S. Department of Health and Human Services
www.healthfinder.gov
Provides information and lists organizations that produce reliable information.

Eating disorders:
National Eating Disorders Association
www.NationalEatingDisorders.org
Information, resources, and links for resolving eating disorders

Something Fishy Website on Eating Disorders
www.something-fishy.org
Offers extensive resources and referrals for eating disorders.

Selected References

American Dietetic Association, American College of Sports Medicine, and Dietitians of Canada. "Joint Position Statement: Nutrition and Athletic Performance." *Journal of the American Dietetic Association.* 12: 1543–56, 2000.

Association of International Marathon Medical Directors Statement on Fluids. http://www.medicalnewstoday.com/medicalnews.php?newsis = 50087

Berardi, J., T. Price, E. Noreen and P. Lemon. "Postexercise Muscle Glycogen Recovery Enhanced with a Carbohydrate-Protein Supplement." *Med Sci Sports Exerc 38,* (6):1106-1113, 2006.

Beals, K. and M. Manore. "Behavioral, Psychological, and Physical Characteristics of Female Athletes with Subclinical Eating Disorders." *International Journal of Sports Nutrition and Exercise Metabolism.* 10, (2):128–43, 2000.

Brouns, F., W. Saris, and N. Rehrer. "Abdominal Complaints and Gastro-Intestinal Function During Long-Lasting Exercise." *International Journal of Sports Medicine.* 8 :175–89, 1987.

Bouchard, C., et al. "The Response to Long Term Overeeding in Identical Twins." *New England Journal of Medicine.* 322:1477–82, 1990.

Burke, L. "Nutritional Needs for Exercise in the Heat." *Comparative Biochemistry and Physiology Part* A 128, no. 4:735–48, 2001.

Carrithers, J.A., et al. "Effects of Post-Exercise Protein-Carbohydrate Feedings on Muscle Glycogen Restoration." *Journal of Applied Physiology.* 88, no. 6:1976–82, 2000.

Casa, D., et al. "National Athletic Trainers' Association Position Statement: Fluid Replacement for Athletes." *Journal of Athletic Training.* 35, no. 2: 212–24, 2000.

Clark, N., M. Nelson, and W. Evans. "Nutrition Education for Elite Women Runners." *Physician and Sportsmedicine.* 16 (2): 124–34, 1988.

Garner, D. "The Effects of Starvation on Behavior: Implications for Dieting and Eating Disorders." *Healthy Weight Journal.* 12 (5): 68–72, 1998.

Hagberg, J., et al. "Determinants of Body Composition in Post-Menopausal Women." *Journal of Gerontology.* Series A—Biol Sci Med Sci 55 (10): M607–12, 2000.

Hill, R.J. and P.S. Davies. "The Validity of Self-Reported Energy Intake as Determined Using the Doubly Labeled Water Technique." *British Journal of Nutrition.* 85 (4): 415–30, 2001.

Ivy, J. H. Goforth, B. Damon, T. McCauley, E. Parsons, and T. Price. "Early post-exercise muscle glycogen recovery is enhanced with a carbohdyrate-protein supplement." *J Appl Physiol* 93(4):1337-1344, 2002.

Jakicic, J., et al. "American College of Sports Medicine Position Stand. Appropriate Intervention Strategies for Weight Loss and Prevention of Weight Regain for Adults." *Medicine and Science in Sports and Exercise.* 12: 2145–56, 2001.

Lichtenstein, A. et al. "Diet and Lifestyle Recommendation Revision 2006: A Scientific Statement From the American Heart Association Nutrition Committee." *Circulation* 2006; 114:82-96, 2006.

Malcsewska, J., G. Raczynski, and R. Stupnicki. "Iron Status in Female Endurance Athletes and Non-Athletes." *International Journal of Sports Nutrition and Exercise Metabolism.* 10 (3): 260–76, 2000.

Nativ, A. "Stress Fractures and Bone Health in Track and Field Athletes." *Journal of Science and Medicine in Sport.* 3 (3):268–79, 2000.

Pedersen, A., et al. "Menstrual Differences Due to Vegetarian and Non-Vegetarian Diets." *American Journal of Clinical Nutrition.* 53: 879–85, 1991.

Pendergast, D., J. Leddy, and J. Veentkatraman. "A Perspective on Fat Intake in Athletes." *Journal of the American College of Nutrition.* 19 (3): 345–50, 2000.

Rehrer, N. "Fluid and Electrolyte Balance in Ultra-Endurance Sport." *Sports Medicine.* 31 (10): 701–15, 2001.

Sanborn, C.F., B. Albrecht, and W. Wagner. "Athletic Amenorrhea: Lack of Association with Body Fat." *Medicine and Science in Sports and Exercise.* 19 (3): 207–12, 1987.

Sanborn, C.F., et al. "Disordered Eating and the Female Athlete Triad." *Clinical Sports Medicine.* 19 (2): 199–213, 2000.

Schulz, L.O., et al. "Energy Expenditure of Elite Female Runners Measured by Respiratory Chamber and Doubly Labeled Water." *Journal of Applied Physiology.* 72 (1): 23–28, 1992.

Sherman, W.M. "Muscle Glycogen Supercompensation During the Week Before Athletic Competition." *Sports Science Exchange* (The Gatorade Institute). 2 (16): 1989.

Wilmore, J., et al. "Is There Energy Conservation in Amenorrheic Compared with Eumenorrheic Distance Runners?" *Journal of Applied Physiology.* 72 (1): 15–22, 1992.

Wyatt, HR et al. "Long-term weight loss and breakfast in subjects in the National Weight Control Registry." *Obes Research.* 10(2)78-82, 2002.

Zelasko, C. "Exercise for Weight Loss: What Are the Facts?" *Journal of the American Dietetic Association.* 95:1414–17, 1995.

Photo and Illustration Credits:

Index

EAT WELL – STAY FIT

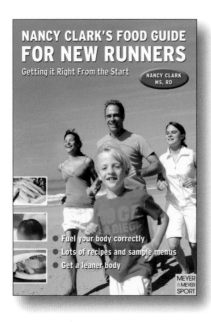

Nancy Clark, MS, RD
Nancy Clark's Food Guide for New Runners
Getting it Right From the Start

New runners can learn how to reach their goals with energy
to spare. This easy-to-read book offers practical tips and
debunks nutrition myths. Eating on the run, fueling and
weight management are all topics that are discussed.
Healthy recipes and sample menus are included.

160 pages, full-color print, 50 photos, 53 charts
Paperback, 6 1/2" x 9 1/4"
ISBN: 9781841262628
$ 16.95 US/$ 29.95 AUS/£ 12.95 UK/€ 16.95

Gloria Averbuch/Nancy Clark, RD
Food Guide for Soccer
Tips & Recipes from the Pros

Soccer athletes are hungry for good nutrition information.
This easy-to-read book offers practical tips, debunks
nutrition myths, and is a simple "how to" resource for soccer
players, their coaches and parents. Professional soccer
players offer advice along with recipes and sample menus.

224 p., full-color print, 48 photos, 11 illus., 29 charts
Paperback, 6 1/2" x 9 1/4"
ISBN: 9781841262888
$ 18.95 US/$ 32.95 AUS/£ 14.95 UK/€ 18.95

All books available as E-books
– secure & user-friendly

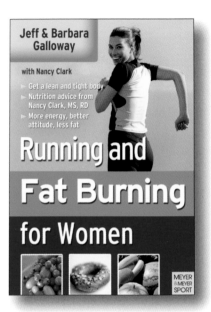

Jeff & Barbara Galloway
Running & Fat Burning for Women

Couch potatoes and seasoned exercisers alike can improve wellbeing by implementing eating strategies and gentle segments of exercise. Learn about the process of fat deposition and burning, and how to gain control over both sides of the issue: intake and burn-off.

2nd Edition, 200 p., full-color print, 30 photos
Paperback, 6 ¹/₂" x 9 ¹/₄"
ISBN: 9781841262437
$ 17.95 US/$ 32.95 AUS/£ 14.95 UK/€ 16.95

Ironman Edition
Ingrid Loos Miller
Weight Management for Triathletes
When Training Is Not Enough

This guide provides practical information and tools that will help triathletes of all levels in their quest to improve body composition for performance and aesthetics while enjoying a multi-dimensional life. Strategies for various eating styles for men and women are offered.

200 p., full-color print, 58 photos, 6 illus., 16 charts
Paperback, 6 ¹/₂" x 9 ¹/₄"
ISBN: 9781841262901
$ 18.95 US/$ 32.95 AUS/£ 14.95 UK/€ 18.95

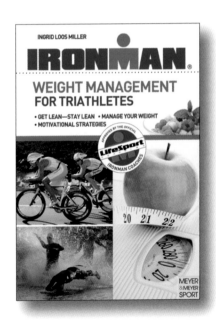

For further titles go to www.m-m-sports.com

■ online
www.m-m-sports.com

■ E-Mail
sales@m-m-sports.com

MEYER
& MEYER
SPORT